RAISING CHILD

An exploration of family online social media networking experiences

Suzana Stipanovic

Table of Contents

List of Abbreviations

ABS	Australian Bureau of Statistics
AIFS	Australian Institute of Family Studies
ACT	Australian Capital Territory
EC	Early Childhood
ECA	Early Childhood Australia
ECE	Early Childhood Education
NSW	New South Whales
MM	Mamma Mia
NT	Northern Territory
RCN	Raising Children Network
RQ	Research Questions
SA	South Australia
SIDE	Social Identity model of Deindividualization Effects
QLD	Queensland
TAS	Tasmania
UN	United Nations
US	United States
Vic	Victoria
WA	Western Australia

Glossary of Terms

Blog: A narrative published online.

Blogger: An individual who writes and publishes narratives online.

Cyber community: A group of individuals interacting online within a specific forum or website.

Early Childhood Educators: for the purposes of this thesis, this term refers to all types of early childhood staff regardless of their qualifications and job responsibilities.

Forum: An online discussion board featuring one or more categories or topics for discussion.

Mamma Mia: An online parenting website targeting mothers with young children.

Mummy blogs: Blogs about the personal experiences of motherhood written by mothers.

Nethnographers: Researchers studying online communities and how they are influenced by the interactions and interconnections between those who have joined or posted a note in the forum.

Online community culture: Patterns of exchanges and interactions expected and accepted within an online community.

Post: A message posted in an online forum.

Postings: Various messages posted in an online forum.

Raising Children Network (RCN): An online parenting website targeting individuals raising children from birth to sixteen years of age.

Thread: A list of online messages connected to a particular idea/issue/question.

List of Figures

List of Tables

Abstract

Australian families raising children today are turning to the internet for parenting information and support. As the wellbeing of children and families is connected with the support families receive (Grace, Hayes, & Wise, 2017), research into online support being accessed by families with children is warranted. Content analysis of postings on the online forums within the Raising Children Network over a six-month period was conducted to ascertain insights about respondents' interests regarding raising children in Australia today. To gain further insights into how participation in social networking sites may influence family experiences, parents utilising social media were also invited to complete an online survey. Online behaviours such as passive support and cyber lurking were found within the online forum postings analysed, and were also reported by the survey respondents. These findings can inform those managing online parenting networks about aspects that require better monitoring and moderation of participation in social media forums aimed at supporting those raising children today. These findings can also be used by educators to advise and assist families in early childhood settings to adopt a variety of strategies for online interactions, optimise the potential social supports available through social media, and enhance knowledge sharing within cyber communities.

Chapter 1. Introduction

1.1 Organisation of the Chapter

Australian families are using information and communication technologies for networking and seeking support regarding family matters. According to the Australian Bureau of Statistics (ABS), 86 percent of all families now have access to the internet at home (ABS, 2016). This is an increase of 83 percent from 2012-13 (ABS, 2016), virtually eliminating some of the social and geographic barriers historically isolating many families. Electronic social networks can now transmit social support traditionally only offered in face-to-face encounters (Bambina, 2007). In fact, an ethnographic turn is occurring whereby virtual communities are forming online (Rouleau, de Rond, & Musca, 2014), as socially isolated parents living in urban communities too (Drentea & Moren-Cross, 2005) are turning to the internet to connect with others. This shift to virtual ethnographies (Rouleau, de Rond, & Musca, 2014) introduces new communication media for and barriers to the effective exchange and provisions of social and informational support (Doty & Dworkin, 2014) via online access. Thus, research regarding specific matters that families are investigating online through social networking and parental experiences of online social media is warranted.

This chapter introduces the context of the study presented in this thesis. The first section identifies contemporary family trends encompassing the adoption of online social networking systems, based on a socio-ecological conceptualisation of their children's place within an exosystem (Bronfenbrenner, 2009). The second section introduces the online social network community that was examined for the purposes of this research. The third section explains the significance of this study, and asserts the need for further research and implications regarding how online family social networks could be better designed to more effectively communicate credible child development information to families. The final section outlines the contents of the remaining chapters of this thesis.

1

1.2 Information seeking and online social networking

Seeking information and support as a parent is complicated - particularly during transitions from pregnancy to early motherhood (Davis, 2015). Today, information seeking online is a part of parenting, in particular for parents whose children are in the care of doctors and nurses while in intensive care (Davis, 2015). Families where the parents are engaged in paid employment are often unable to access community support programs during business hours. According to Hall and Irvine (2009), these families are finding that online support groups mitigate their feelings of isolation. Furthermore, as society becomes increasingly mobile, parents are less able to speak with friends and relatives on a daily basis (Pedersen & Smithson, 2010). Simultaneously, virtual communities (Drentea & Moren-Cross, 2005) appear to have become surrogate psychosocial support networks for young families online (Hall & Irvine, 2009).

Today, family matters blogs, Twitter feeds, and virtual social networks are available on a plethora of websites and social media pages. Online blogs and social networking have formed virtual worlds for online users, and are a new research platform for researchers of virtual communities (Mukherji & Albon, 2014); and these latter have been described by Rouleau et al. (2014) as "nethnographers" (p. 3).

An example of an Australian parenting website is *the Raising Children Network* (http://raisingchildren.net.au/), which is a highly regarded Australian website designed to provide families with research-based information about family life and child development. Resources such as online forums, podcasts, webinars, and videos are available to users of the *Raising Children Network* (RCN).

1.3 Typology of social support

Three categories distinguish a traditional offline typology for social support. These comprise emotional support, informational support, and instrumental support (Evans, Donelle, & Hume-Loveland, 2012). Emotional support encompasses affection, concern, comforting and encouragement. Informational support includes provision of knowledge, information and advice. Instrumental support involves more tangible assistance such as help with daily chores or childminding (Evans et al., 2012). The assimilation of such offline social supports was used to develop an online social support typology that was categorised in five ways as: informational support; esteem support; tangible support; network support; and emotional support (Evans et al., 2012). New forms of social capital were also formed through discussion groups which can increase the generation of social connections. A discourse analysis of an online mothering discussion board found that users experienced an increase in social capital through the provision of informational support, community building, and emotional support (Evans et al., 2012).

This present study analysed content contributed by online community members of a moderated discussion forum designed to support families raising children. A purposive sample of active posts between January and June 2016 were selected from the parenting website, the *Raising Children Network*' (RCN), and analysed. The second stage involved an online survey questionnaire targeting families participating in online parenting communities.

The aim of this study was to capture parents' perceptions about their children's early childhood experiences before starting school, as depicted through the parents' participation in social media. These perceptions reflect parents' values and beliefs about parenting during early childhood, as well as their satisfaction and concerns about the use of non-parental EC services. To date, studies about parents' involvement in EC services have not been explored through their use of social media to ascertain parents' perceptions about children's growth and development, education, health and wellbeing and any other matters of interest during early childhood. Findings of the present study aim to contribute new insights to extend our knowledge and understanding about contemporary parents' perspectives on raising children in Australia today.

1.4. Scope and aims of the study

This study focuses on the online social networking experiences of parents residing in Australia. The aim of this study was to gain further insights into what issues parents discussed through online social media, whether they found this information to be reliable and useful, and how they used it, if at all. The study also aimed to gain insights into whether online interactions amongst parents within a parenting community have influenced child and family experiences in the real world. Thus, the two research questions (RQ) underpinning this study were defined as follows:

RQ 1: What topics or issues regarding raising children matters are reflected in Australian parents' online social networking interactions?

RQ 2: How has participation in social media networks influenced parents' perspectives about raising children matters?

1.5. Significance of the study

While there have been several international studies on online social networking experiences of parents (Daneback & Plantin, 2015; Plantin & Daneback, 2009), such studies in Australia are scarce (Davis, 2015). With a growing number of families turning to the internet for information and social support, it is imperative that the use and effectiveness of this medium's potential to offer information as well as to create social capital is explored. This is particularly important for families who may be replacing support once received face-to-face with online support. The level of anonymity afforded to online users (Christopherson, 2007) in the past has been found to restrict or inhibit effective information exchange and emotional support (Drentea & Moren-Cross, 2005).

Conversely, online anonymity has enabled some users to experiment with aggressive and negative behaviours that they may not typically portray in face-to-face discussions (Christopherson, 2007). In fact, McDaniel, Coyne, and Holmes (2012) found that negative online social networking experiences may compromise family wellbeing. Given that child and family experiences and outcomes are influenced by available parental information and social support (Grace, Hayes, & Wise, 2017), research on online social networking experiences of Australian parents is warranted.

1.6. Organisation of the thesis

This thesis is comprised of six chapters. Chapter 1 provides an introduction to the study, situating it within the landscape of social networking available for access to parents. It introduces the contemporary shift in how communities once defined by geography are now defined by membership of an online network (Rouleau et al., 2014). This shift brings with it not only new ways of offering information and support on parenting, and thereby creating a new form of social capital, but also identifies barriers to overcome that would enable the effective provision of information and support that parents are seeking online.

Chapter 2 provides a review of the literature based on local and international research on online cyber communities, in particular on cyber networking, and identifies gaps in the research which this study aims to address. Chapter 3 discusses the research methods employed in this study to investigate the two research questions identified above.

Chapter 4 presents the study findings in two parts. The first part presents the findings from the first stage of the research – the content analysis of the posts studied from within the RCN forums. The second part presents the findings from the online survey distributed, which encompasses the second stage of the research, which presents: the survey respondents' characteristics; perspectives on ECE; social media reliability and effectiveness for gaining information and social support.

Chapter 5 provides a discussion making links between findings from the content analysis and the online survey. Chapter 6 addresses the two research questions in light of the findings of the study. The limitations of the study and recommendations for future research are also presented in this chapter. Recommendations for policies and user guidelines that can improve the level of information and social support parents can receive through participation in online parenting communities are also provided. The thesis concludes with recommendations for how the research findings from this study can assist parents and social media providers with knowledge about the better use of online social media for parenting purposes.

1.7. Chapter summary

This chapter has introduced the notion that contemporary Australian families are turning to online social media as a source for information and support. The aims and scope of the study have been presented, along with the significance of the study, emphasising the importance of optimising online social networking experiences and outcomes for individuals raising children in Australia. A review of relevant literature in relation to the themes of the study is presented next in Chapter 2.

Chapter 2. Literature Review

This chapter presents an analysis of key literature addressing family online social networking sites and experiences. The procedure adopted in researching the literature is outlined, and a brief synopsis of the main themes emerging from the analysis is presented. By focusing on family social networking and its impact on child and family social capital, commonalities across issues found within the literature are presented, together with gaps in the research undertaken, in affirming the need for the present study.

2.1 Researching the literature

This literature review is based on research sourced from academic library databases covering items written and published in English. Database searches were refined using subject key words comprising: social sciences; education; humanities; psychology; and Australia. This yielded results for relevant databases ultimately selected, comprising A+ Education; ERIC; Education Research Complete; PsycINFO; Scopus; Taylor and Francis online; and Wiley online library. In addition to these databases, online journal articles were directly searched, as were EBSCOhost and Google Scholar. Key words searched in the library databases comprised: parenting; day care; childcare; child care; preschool; kindergarten; internet; online; networking; social media; online networking; online communities; virtual communities; virtual ethnography; blogs; parenting blogs; and social networking. Relevant scholarly articles were also studied, and additional articles were retrieved from these as well.

2.2 Uri Bronfenbrenner's social ecology model

Bronfenbrenner's model of social ecology explains how various contexts both influence and impact families and, consequently, child development (Bowes & Grace, 2009), and how children and families also impact and influence other families and communities (Grace et al., 2017).

Figure 1. Bronfenbrenner's Social Ecology Model

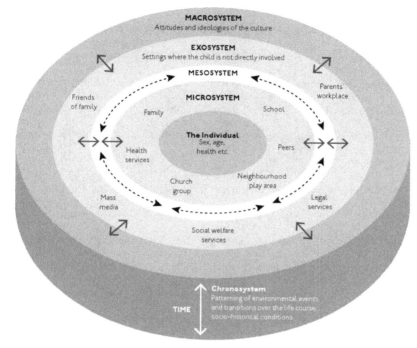

(from Grace, Hayes, & Wise, 2017, p. 6)

Family social capital can be developed through relationships amongst the immediate and extended family and with others in the community (Bowes, Watson, & Pearson, 2012). Interactions occurring between children and parents within the microsystem affect the child's macrosystem, which is in turn influenced by community cultures, beliefs and values (September, Rich, & Roman, 2016). Nested within the exosystem, family networks can also play a pivotal role in children's learning and development (Bronfenbrenner, 2009). In Western contemporary societies such as Australia, online social media communities have increasingly become a part of a child's exosystem in the new millennium.

Immune to social and geographic barriers previously isolating some families (Drentea & Moren-Cross, 2005; Evans et al., 2012; Nieuwboer, Fukkink, & Hermanns, 2013), online social media is not only networking individuals but also interjecting and projecting cultural attitudes and ideologies onto families on a mass scale (Bambina, 2007). Social support positively supports women during pregnancy, birth and the postnatal period, and has a negative correlation with postpartum depression (Evans et al., 2012). There is a growing potential for further accommodation of social support and social capital (Bartholomew, Schoppe-Sullivan, Glassman, Kamp Dush, & Sullivan, 2012) through the internet, in particular when available psychosocial supports are inadequate for meeting the needs of contemporary young families (Hall & Irvine, 2009).

A great deal of online information is targeted at parents or expectant parents (Daneback & Plantin, 2015). In their study, Drentea and Moren-Cross (2005) reported that virtual communities formed by parents with young children can offer social capital, in particular for mothers in the early stages of motherhood, which is in general the period of greatest physical and social isolation. Women who accessed online social support during pregnancy reported a more pleasant first year of motherhood, and their children were found to be happier and healthier seven years on (Drentea & Moren-Cross, 2005). Accuracy and reliability of information on the internet is, therefore, important, especially when this information can directly influence families and impact children's life experiences. Interconnections and interactions between online forum participants play an important role in encouraging and supporting forum members (Pedersen & Smithson, 2010). Further research exploring the topical information that parents as active members of cyber communities are searching for online, and their experiences of online interactions, is therefore warranted.

2.3 Current research on parent online social networking

Many websites offer parents health information and social networking opportunities (Daneback & Plantin, 2015). A positive correlation between internet use and capacity building has been made (Evans et al., 2012). Research on online parenting networks exists (Daneback & Plantin, 2015; Davis, 2015; Drentea & Moren-Cross, 2005; Hall & Irvine, 2009; Madge & O'Connor,

9

2006; Nieuwboer et al., 2013; Pedersen & Smithson, 2010; Sarkadi & Bremberg, 2005). However, these studies reflect a digital gender divide, with advantaged women dominating parenting cyberspaces (Madge & O'Connor, 2006; Pedersen & Smithson, 2010; Sarkadi & Bremberg, 2005). For instance, despite Sweden's strong social policies bridging the gender gap, Sarkadi and Bremberg (2005) found, surprisingly, that only 5 percent of respondents in the internet-based parenting support site studied were men.

Madge and O'Connor (2006) conducted a study to gain more understanding of the evolution of parenting practices by new and/or expectant mothers seeking child health information online. The study researched dialogue between mothers, predominately characterised as middle-class women, and nurses on a website operated by two mothers from the U.K., which found a significant reinforcement of traditional gender roles throughout many of the discussion forums. Pedersen and Smithson (2010) studied the British internet site 'mumsnet', an online community which is 'naturally' characterised by its title. Davis (2015) also studied online social interconnections and information sharing between new mothers who interacted within Australian 'mummy' blogs. Such studies have found users of online parenting forums and blogs to have forged friendships and interactions that have extended beyond the cyberspace (Davis, 2015; Hall & Irvine, 2009).

In a bid to identify parental outreach for information, Nichols (2014) examined parenting research into learning and development activities for young children. This study found a gender discrepancy in regard to outsourcing parenting information from within the wider community. The study reports that some fathers found that much of the child information was targeted at middle-class Australian women. It was further reported that much of the information was promoting child learning and development activities. This finding, of online media mostly targeting middle-class women, is consistent with research by Madge and O'Connor (2006) and Sarkadi and Bremberg (2005), who found that social networking was being employed to a large extent by advantaged, educated women who were technologically proficient.

Research targeting fathers seeking information about children's behaviours and other topics searched for online is, however, scarce (Daneback & Plantin, 2015). Bartholomew et al. (2012) recruited a purposive sample of 154 women and 150 men who were online users of Facebook and transitioning to parenthood. Although the study included an almost equal representation of male and female participants, a higher proportion of the women were found to utilise the site for parenting information than the men.

Drentea and Moren-Cross (2005) studied an online community specifically made up of expectant mothers or mothers within the very early stages of motherhood. Although the presence of both men and women was found on parenting websites, it is clear from a review of this literature that community members were predominantly female. Hall and Irvine (2009) suggest that the marginalisation of men on such websites can impact fathers and influence them to withdraw from active parenting. With many studies researching user interactions on online social networking sites that were occupied mostly by either expectant mums or mothers of young children, there is a need for research on interactions and information sourced by any person raising a child – including foster caregivers who are allocated to raise children by the State when biological parents are assessed as being unable to do so. This is particularly important because of concerns about raising children for those who are not biologically their parents (Lansford, Ceballo, Abbey, & Stewart, 2001).

2.4 Family utilisation of ECE services.

Quality Early Childhood Education (ECE) has been found to be an important long term contributor to human development and well-being (Maguire & Hayes, 2012; September et al., 2016). However, not all families access ECE settings for their children (Baxter & Hand, 2013). O'Connor et al. (2016) studied attendance rates of preschool children, and found that vulnerable children and families experience certain barriers to accessing ECE. Berry et al. (2016) found that full-time high quality child care can be a buffer for children from low socio-economic family backgrounds. Marshall, Robeson, Tracy, Frye, and Roberts (2013) have also found that maternal employment can moderate the cycle of children living in poverty, with subsidised child care being a mediating factor.

Child health and development is better facilitated within formal ECE programs; however, families unable to access fee subsidies were found to rely on informal care which was of lower quality than formal ECE services (Marshall et al., 2013). It was also found that Aboriginal and Torres Strait Islander children and children with English as a second language were less likely to access formal ECE settings (Maguire & Hayes, 2012).

Baxter and Hand (2013) found that some families who do not experience such barriers still choose not to use formal ECE or non-parental care. Conversely, Coley, Lombardi, Sims, and Votruba-Drzal (2013) found that Australian mothers who were aware of the developmental benefits of ECE were accessing ECE for their children regardless of their employment status. Research into whether such parents are sharing this view with their peers online is warranted. Indeed, access to ECE from birth is embedded within a child's rights under the United Nations (UN) Convention on the Rights of the Child (Ancheta Arrabal, 2015; UN, 1989). However, current Australian government policy, funding placements only for children whose parents are working, studying or looking for work (Australian Government, 2016), is likely to challenge families exercising this right for their children.

Studies of online interactions between families may provide insights on whether Australian families are beginning to accept or challenge this government policy as compromising the rights for all children to access ECE. Research on the impact of maternal education rates reveals the benefits of ECE for child development. Craig and Powell (2013) found that mothers in the paid workforce spent the same amount of time with their children as did mothers who stayed at home, and that they achieved this by multitasking, scaling back on housework, and reducing personal leisure time. In fact, mothers working full time were found to be maintaining conversations with their children by engaging in activities such as reading with their children, to ensure their children were not missing out on interactions with their

12

mothers, care and nurturing (Craig & Powell, 2013). These findings highlight the need to investigate whether this information is made available to families via online parenting websites.

Governments around the world have been using a variety of strategies to promote the importance of ECE. For instance, Baxter and Hand (2013) found that Sweden achieved high rates of attendance in ECE services following a 70-year campaign educating families that ECE was a child's right regardless of parental engagement in paid employment. In Norway, 80 percent of children aged between 12 months and two years attend ECE settings (Britt Drugli & Mari Undheim, 2012). Fenech (2013) encourages educators to openly discuss utilisation of ECE with families and promote the developmental benefits it provides children. In the United States (US), families were more likely to access full time ECE for their children at a younger age due to poor social policy and welfare systems resulting in maternal need to return to paid work soon after the birth of a child (Baxter & Hand, 2013). Government policy in Estonia provides maternity leave with full pay, enabling mothers or fathers to stay at home with their babies until they are two years of age. However, research conducted by Veisson (2015) found significant shortages of ECE placements for toddlers under the age of two, with families actively seeking short-term play-centre care, and often settling for half-day care due to lack of availability. Findings such as this reinforce the importance of further research to ascertain a better understanding of parents' needs of and perspectives on accessing ECE for their children.

2.5 Families and educators as stakeholders in ECE

When educators work with families and the community to advocate for equity of access to ECE for all children, community appreciation for the developmental benefits of ECE and care will heighten (Ionescu, 2015). Fordham, Gibson, and Bowes (2012) found that families desire the empowerment that services can facilitate by providing information and support (particularly in advocating for continual improvement). Jackiewicz, Saggers, and Frances (2011) define "*horizontal equity*" as the capacity to equitably provide a service to a community with similar needs; however, they found that few services were able to offer *"vertical equity"*, i.e. adjust service delivery to meet the special needs of certain groups such as Indigenous families. Research conducted by Irvine, Davidson, Veresov, Adams, and Devi (2015) found that the majority of families accessing ECE fell into one of two categories. The first is the *Service User*. As a service user, the parent adopts a passive role in the use of the service, by assuming that the service is operating within regulatory requirements. The second category is the *Consumer Concept* category. It is said that parents in this category believe that their involvement in the service will enhance the quality of care afforded to their child.

Correlations between living in a remote community, low family education levels, and low ECE participation, were found for Indigenous children (Biddle, 2007). Jackiewicz et al. (2011) also found that Indigenous families were more critical of early learning services that did not acknowledge their family's Indigenous heritage. Furthermore, Indigenous families preferred that Indigenous educators teach their children about their cultural heritage. Research into whether Indigenous children from rural and remote communities experience greater participation in early learning services that are characterised as having a greater proportion of Aboriginal and Torres Strait Islander educators is warranted.

2.6 The bystander effect and its transfer into the digital community

Latané and Darley (1970) hypothesised 'the bystander effect' following failures in helping behaviours of least 38 bystanders who witnessed an assailant attack their neighbour, Kitty Genovese. Kitty's neighbours watched the attack for over half an hour without calling the police. The attack ultimately led to Kitty's murder. Following this tragic event, to explain the apathy of onlookers, various theories were proposed to suggest that anonymity and alienation came with individuals living in big cities and reduced individuals' sense of responsibility for one another (Latané & Darley, 1970).

To investigate this further, Latané and Darley (1970) interviewed Kitty's neighbours, and found findings to the contrary. Kitty's neighbours attested that they were horrified at what was happening and were concerned immensely for her safety. They explained that they had in fact helped one another out in previous emergency situations. In order to determine what conditions enabled helping behaviours and what conditions inhibited them, Latané and Darley (1970) conducted laboratory and field experiments. By simulating a fire in the building (Latane & Darley, 1968) or a robbery in a liquor store, Latané & Darley (1970) found that individuals experienced a diffusion of responsibility (Latané & Nida, 1981) when multiple bystanders were present during the emergency situation. That is, when a bystander was alone at the onset of a perceived emergency, they presented helping behaviours (Latané & Darley, 1970). However, when multiple bystanders were present, most people failed to render assistance, maintaining the expectation that one of the other bystanders would eventually enact (Latané & Darley, 1970).

Anker and Feeley (2011), furthermore, draw on the expression, "pluralistic ignorance" (p. 14), to describe the process by which bystanders look to one another in order to deem a situation as critical and to determine whether or not to enact helping behaviours. Scaffidi Abbate, Boca, Spadaro, and Romano (2014) describe the bystander effect as a phenomenon whereby the likelihood of someone rendering aid or assistance to someone in distress is reduced as the number of physical bystanders is increased. Their study further researched the implicit bystander effect, which describes how the mere imagining of the presence of others can reduce helping behaviour.

Innovations in the digital arena have revolutionised human interaction (Wong-Lo & Bullock, 2014). The very anonymous nature of online social interactions affords users a greater deal of autonomy in experimenting with new behaviours without the fear of experiencing the social consequences they could otherwise experience with family or friends (Christopherson, 2007). One could argue that the anonymity afforded by internet use, and users being privy to the number of likes, views or followers for certain posts (Polder-Verkiel, 2012), can exponentially reduce bystander helping behaviours (Scaffidi Abbate, Boca, Spadaro, & Romano, 2014).

Polder-Verkiel (2012) found bystander behaviours on online social networking sites. Their study examined the case of nineteen-year-old Abraham Biggs, who publicly broadcast intentional self-harm by webcam on a forum watched by up to 1,500 viewers. Abraham described the lethal concoction of drugs that he would be taking on the forum, saying: "I'll be dead within a few hours" (p. 122). Of the 1,500 viewers, only 4 eventually called for emergency assistance, albeit too late – Abraham's body was found by Miami police officers several hours after his death (Polder-Verkiel, 2012). Thus, it is found that traditional bystander behaviours (Latané & Darley, 1970) transmit into contemporary cyber communities (Polder-Verkiel, 2012), forming a digital bystander culture (Wong-Lo & Bullock, 2014). Such bystander behaviours could present as 'cyber lurking' (Pedersen & Smithson, 2010) and/or offers only of passive support (Drentea & Moren-Cross, 2005). Furthermore, one could argue that a diffusion of responsibility (Latané & Nida, 1981) could be exponentially increased within cyber communities, which are usually characterised by high numbers of members due to the accessible nature of the online environment (Polder-Verkiel, 2012).

Although several studies have examined online parental interactions within cyber communities (Davis, 2015; Doty & Dworkin, 2014), much of this research has focused on mother-centred online interactions (Drentea & Moren-Cross, 2005; Hall & Irvine, 2009). To date, there is little Australian research exploring the experiences of fathers and mothers raising children in this country. Researches such as those by Krieg, Smith, and Davis (2014) and Davis (2015) have looked at the exchange of information amongst mothers with young babies through blogs and social media. There is, however, little research on identifying supports for and barriers to effective user interconnections within parenting cyber communities for both mothers and fathers. Such research could assist in identifying the levels of support, interconnections, and satisfaction with the timely nature of emotional and social support sought and received by those accessing these websites.

2.7 Theoretical underpinnings of the study

This section provides the theoretical underpinnings that shape this research (Cooksey & McDonald, 2009). As depicted in Figure 2, the combination of the Social Ecology theory of Bronfenbrenner (2009) and the model of the Bystander Effect by Latané and Darley (1970) has influenced the design and analysis of this study.

The combined use of Bronfenbrenner (2009) and Latané and Darley (1970) enabled the exploration of family online social networking experiences of raising children matters. It is suggested that interconnections within cyber communities can influence knowledge, support and social capital available to families, and that this can impact children's early experiences and long-term developmental outcomes. For the purposes of this research, social media networking sits within the exosystem of Bronfenbrenner's social ecological system theory. Latane and Darley's bystander effect model depicts engagement and lack of engagement in supportive behaviours in different contexts. The aim of the present study is to understand the development of social capital achieved through engagement of supportive behaviours through online social networking.

Figure 2. Theoretical Framework underpinning this study

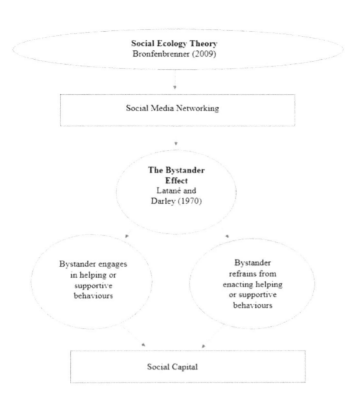

2.8 Chapter summary

This chapter presented an analysis of relevant local and international literature, discussing research in the area of parental use of internet-based resources for information and emotional support. It introduced the theoretical underpinnings of this study, based on the work of Bronfenbrenner (2009) and Latané and Darley (1970), which enable this study, situated within social media networking, to be examined from the perspective of a child and family exosystem operating within the context of a virtual community. The methodologies employed to address the research questions in this study are discussed in the next Chapter.

Chapter 3. Methodology

This Chapter describes the methodology employed in this study. The study approach, design measures and tests for validity are also presented. Furthermore, procedures for data collection and analysis are discussed, before describing demographic characteristics of the sample of respondents involved in this study.

3.1 Approach to the study

Adopting a mixed methods research approach (Johnson & Christensen, 2014), this study comprised two stages of data collection to address the two key research questions being investigated. Stage One involved a thematic analysis of online forum discussions of a parenting website, namely, the Raising Children Network (RCN) (www.raisingchildren.net.au). The second Stage of the study involved a parent survey aimed at families who used online social media for parenting purposes. This research was informed by focusing on children's relationships as conceptualised within a social ecological framework (Bronfenbrenner, 2009). This theory illustrates how interactions within and between a child's family and community can impact family wellbeing as well as children's developmental and learning outcomes (Grace et al., 2017). Thus, a particular focus was placed on the use of family social media networks on the internet, and on whether such online interactions assisted families raising children and possibly impacted their children's early childhood experiences.

Ethnography involves the study of a group of people and the gaining of insights about their perspectives, patterns of interaction, values and attitudes (Johnson & Christensen, 2014). During the current era of the internet and the plethora of social media sites that have emerged with it, ethnographers have shifted from studying a group of individuals defined by their geographic location (Johnson & Christensen, 2014) to that of a group of individuals defined by their membership of an online community (Rouleau et al., 2014). Online communities form what Czarniawska (2014) refers to as "virtual ethnographies"(p. 70). The collection and analysis of posts on the Raising Children Network provided a "holistic description" (p. 50) of

19

family backgrounds. Marshall, Robeson, Tracy, Frye, and Roberts (2013) have also found that maternal employment can moderate the cycle of children living in poverty, with subsidised child care being a mediating factor.

Child health and development is better facilitated within formal ECE programs; however, families unable to access fee subsidies were found to rely on informal care which was of lower quality than formal ECE services (Marshall et al., 2013). It was also found that Aboriginal and Torres Strait Islander children and children with English as a second language were less likely to access formal ECE settings (Maguire & Hayes, 2012).

Baxter and Hand (2013) found that some families who do not experience such barriers still choose not to use formal ECE or non-parental care. Conversely, Coley, Lombardi, Sims, and Votruba-Drzal (2013) found that Australian mothers who were aware of the developmental benefits of ECE were accessing ECE for their children regardless of their employment status. Research into whether such parents are sharing this view with their peers online is warranted. Indeed, access to ECE from birth is embedded within a child's rights under the United Nations (UN) Convention on the Rights of the Child (Ancheta Arrabal, 2015; UN, 1989). However, current Australian government policy, funding placements only for children whose parents are working, studying or looking for work (Australian Government, 2016), is likely to challenge families exercising this right for their children.

Studies of online interactions between families may provide insights on whether Australian families are beginning to accept or challenge this government policy as compromising the rights for all children to access ECE. Research on the impact of maternal education rates reveals the benefits of ECE for child development. Craig and Powell (2013) found that mothers in the paid workforce spent the same amount of time with their children as did mothers who stayed at home, and that they achieved this by multitasking, scaling back on housework, and reducing personal leisure time. In fact, mothers working full time were found to be maintaining conversations with their children by engaging in activities such as reading with their children, to ensure their children were not missing out on interactions with their

12

mothers, care and nurturing (Craig & Powell, 2013). These findings highlight the need to investigate whether this information is made available to families via online parenting websites.

Governments around the world have been using a variety of strategies to promote the importance of ECE. For instance, Baxter and Hand (2013) found that Sweden achieved high rates of attendance in ECE services following a 70-year campaign educating families that ECE was a child's right regardless of parental engagement in paid employment. In Norway, 80 percent of children aged between 12 months and two years attend ECE settings (Britt Drugli & Mari Undheim, 2012). Fenech (2013) encourages educators to openly discuss utilisation of ECE with families and promote the developmental benefits it provides children. In the United States (US), families were more likely to access full time ECE for their children at a younger age due to poor social policy and welfare systems resulting in maternal need to return to paid work soon after the birth of a child (Baxter & Hand, 2013). Government policy in Estonia provides maternity leave with full pay, enabling mothers or fathers to stay at home with their babies until they are two years of age. However, research conducted by Veisson (2015) found significant shortages of ECE placements for toddlers under the age of two, with families actively seeking short-term play-centre care, and often settling for half-day care due to lack of availability. Findings such as this reinforce the importance of further research to ascertain a better understanding of parents' needs of and perspectives on accessing ECE for their children.

2.5 Families and educators as stakeholders in ECE

When educators work with families and the community to advocate for equity of access to ECE for all children, community appreciation for the developmental benefits of ECE and care will heighten (Ionescu, 2015). Fordham, Gibson, and Bowes (2012) found that families desire the empowerment that services can facilitate by providing information and support (particularly in advocating for continual improvement). Jackiewicz, Saggers, and Frances (2011) define *"horizontal equity"* as the capacity to equitably provide a service to a community with similar the potential research group (Johnson & Christensen, 2014), comprising individuals raising children in Australia. This analysis provided an overall view of how a group may come together and interact (Johnson & Christensen, 2014) by sharing their experiences, concerns, and questions about raising children matters in contemporary Australian society.

The research methods used in this study involved the collation of data to gain insights about online conversations and communications between families with children. The study maintained some interest in the frequency of the online interactions as well as the quality and quantity of information gained by individuals participating in social media networks. Online forums are message boards or discussion sites where internet users can post messages and probe other internet users for answers to questions they may have.

The research in Stage One involved doing a content analysis of online forum data within the Raising Children Network (RCN). This network was selected because it is located within a reputable website that is endorsed by the Australian Government Department of Social Services. The RCN offers families with children a plethora of online resources, communication platform and research-based information, and was developed in consultation with over 1000 parents, researchers and experts in child and adolescent health. Information and forum discussions located within the RCN are available to parents with children from birth to 18 years of age. These forms are online message boards enabling participants to post questions and correspond through the internet with others interested in raising children. Although these forums are not quality assured by the RCN, the website promotes ethical use of the forums and specifies the terms and conditions of use, with a moderator facilitating the forum if a participant objects to a user engaging in unacceptable conduct. Apart from this, there appears to be no ongoing public moderation of the RCN forums.

Data analysed on the RCN encompassed posts and replies to posts which occurred across all forums, which were submitted to the website between January and June 2016. The dates were purposefully selected to correspond with the candidature period and the sequence of methodology selected for the study. Data collated from the content analysis in Stage One assisted in the construction of the online survey for parents used in Stage Two. The online survey questionnaire was designed to gather further insights about parents' actual experiences of online social networking. The survey questions included identifying the frequency of use, and rating the usefulness of online information and support obtained by parents raising children in Australia today. These research methods were complementary to one another, and assisted in identifying and validating common patterns in the data analysed (Combs & Onwuegbuzie, 2010).

The internet has transformed communication and information channels employed by many individuals and families. Resorting to online resources for information and advice on raising children is increasing (Davis, 2015). In order to develop an epistemological understanding (Krippendorff, 2012) of information sought online by parents, content analysis methodology was employed, as it has been found to enable unobtrusive study of unstructured data by researchers in the social sciences and humanities (Krippendorff, 2012).

Content analysis is a procedure encompassing the sampling, recording, coding and categorising of data such as digital or printed text (Krippendorff, 2012). Content analysis has been used as a research methodology dating back to the early 1600s (Krippendorff, 2012). It takes empirical inquiry into the meaning of communications and how such communications may influence or affect a society (Krippendorff, 2012). Content analysts may employ either quantitative or qualitative approaches to attain a better understanding of a social phenomenon (Krippendorff, 2012). The decision based on the form of quantitative and/or qualitative research methods is based upon the interests, problems or issues being studied by the researcher (Hsieh & Shannon, 2005). In the present study, the category names emerged gradually as the content evolved (Hsieh & Shannon, 2005). This is important because preconceived categories will not enable the gradual emergence of insights and initiation of a coding scheme (Hsieh & Shannon, 2005) based on the data being analysed.

Research results derived by way of content analysis should be replicable (Krippendorff, 2012). That is, if analysed correctly, the same results would be yielded should the same study be replicated by another researcher (Krippendorff, 2012). In this study, interrater reliability testing was conducted to determine the validity of the results. Two coders were appointed to provide interrater reliability.

Content analysis knowledge and skills shaping this study were based on the work of Krippendorff (2012). When embarking upon research using content analysis techniques, the researcher must form analytical constructs. That is, the researcher must understand the context in which the data was written, and identify any possible changes in perspective should the writer have been affected by alternate variables or conditions. According to Krippendorff (2012), effective content analysis research can yield valid inferences. Deductive inferences will enable the researcher to use their data to make generalisations from one individual onto a larger community. Inductive inferences enable the researcher to use data to project what is found to be a generalised norm from a larger community, onto a particular individual. Abductive inferences are usually of greatest interest to content analysts and enable researchers to predict outcomes based on a common finding. By using abductive inferences, a researcher could hypothesise an alternative outcome should there be a change in a variable or a condition (Krippendorff, 2012). For the purpose of the present study, abductive inferencing was applied to determine the type of support and information parents were seeking online, and the general level of online interactions parents experienced when using social media.

3.2 Design methods, measures and stages

This section describes the study methods and measures, and the two Stages involved in collecting and analysing the data that formed the basis of this study.

3.2.1 Stage 1 - Content analysis of online data

Thematic analysis of the data collected through the RCN was conducted in Stage One of the research study. All active posts between January and June 2016 were collated and categorised under fourteen topics that emerged during the initial analysis. It was found that the title of the post often best described its topic, and these were used to determine the categorisation of the posts in the first instance. During the data extraction process, the number of views (i.e. the number of times the post was opened and read by users) was documented. The date of the original post and the date of the latest reply to the post (within the January to June 2016 period) were also noted.

In order to honour relevance and currency of topics or issues connected with raising children, posts which originated prior to January 2016 were included in the study where users replied to them within the January to June 2016 timeframe. For example, user RC0027 originally posted about the difficulties she was experiencing feeding their 10-month-old child in October, 2015 (prior to the catchment phase). However, user RC0096 replied to that post in March, 2016, which fell inside the catchment period of this research. That is, as the reply occurred within the period of catchment, the full discussion was therefore included in the study. Thus, any activity, including in response to a post, that occurred within the target time period determined the inclusion of the posts analysed in this study. It was found that some posts originating in 2008 were still frequented in 2016. For example, user RC0083 requested ideas for baby names on January 28, 2008, and was still receiving replies on the sixth of June 2016. This is an indication that topics can be relevant and extend the life of a post for up to ten years.

3.2.2 Stage 2 - Online survey questionnaire

Qualtrics software was employed to design and construct an online survey questionnaire (see qualtrics.com.au). The survey was advertised through Early Childhood Australia, the Australian Child and Family Research Centre, and the Raising Children Network. The survey advertisement is provided as Appendix H, and comprises 38 items encompassing open and closed questions, and a checklist, as well as rating scales. The questionnaire was piloted with peer researchers prior to publishing (Johnson & Christensen, 2014) to maximise its usability and took around 20 minutes to complete. A copy of the survey appears as Appendix E. A participation information sheet was provided to survey respondents at the entry portal of the survey, and survey respondents confirmed their consent to partake in the study on a voluntary basis prior to commencing the first item in the survey. A copy of the survey respondent information sheet is available as Appendix F.

The survey was constructed in five parts as follows:

- Part 1: Collated each survey respondent's background characteristics such as gender, location, employment status, number and ages of children; and use of non-parental ECE services.

- Part 2: To address the first research question being explored in this study, questions in this part of the survey focused on the type of information survey respondents discussed in online parenting communities.

- Part 3: Questions in this section explored survey respondents' perspectives on ECE, including perceived benefits of ECE for children's learning and development.

- Part 4: This part was designed to answer the second part of this research question, and find whether respondents' online social networking experiences have impacted their children's early childhood experiences.

- Part 5: Asked survey respondents about their social media experiences and whether they would recommend social networking to other parents.

3.3 Ethical considerations of the study

Ethical considerations regarding internet research recommended by Ess (2002) were studied prior to commencing this research. Careful consideration was made in regard to the collation of retrospective data that are freely accessible on public websites. The Macquarie University Human Research Ethics Committee also considered the ethical aspects of this study, granting approval (Reference: 5201600370) in July 2016 (see Appendix G). The application for ethics approval encompassed aspects including: respondent recruitment; participation requirements; obtaining respondent consent; protecting respondent identity; and safe storage of data.

24

Furthermore, in doing any presentations and publication based on this study, it was noted that pseudonyms will be used when referring to any names of friends, relatives or children that may be identified by users in their posts.

The survey questionnaire was uploaded to the RCN website (see http://tinyurl.com/z6pm2jr) inviting users to partake in this study. Early Childhood Australia (ECA) and the Australian Institute of Family Studies (AIFS) also circulated the advertisement for this study within their networks. The researcher's involvement as a forum user was strictly limited to creating a post to invite users to complete the online survey. This post provided details of the study, approval by the university's human research ethics committee, and the voluntary nature of the study. Survey respondents were reassured that they were free to withdraw from the study at any time without consequence at any stage. This initial invitational post, and incidental correspondence with potential participants on the forums, were expected to observe the terms and conditions of each of the three websites as noted above, at all times.

3.4 Data collection and analysis

In this section the nature of the data collected and the procedures used to collect and analyse the data in Stages one and two of the study are provided. The discussion begins with discussion of the quantitative data followed by the qualitative data. Quantitative data was collated, exported and analysed using statistical software comprising Minitab and Microsoft Excel. Qualitative data was collected, analysed and categorised manually using Kripendoff's content analysis strategies, a full description of which was given in the preceding subsections.

3.4.1 Quantitative data

Data collected in Stage One comprised RCN forum posts active between January and June 2016 across all RCN forums (see http://www.raisingchildren.net.au/forum/). This was made possible by selecting the tab entitled 'latest', which indiscriminately produced all the latest posts to any forum to which they may have been originally posted. This approach to the research was taken to ensure that the study captured the voices of all active RCN users between January and June 2016, in particular because certain users may have posted to more than one forum and others may have felt obliged to confine themselves to a particular forum (i.e. indigenous parents; step parents). It is acknowledged that some users may fit into more than one category; thus, capturing all active posts between January and June 2016 across all forums would capture the target audience regardless of which forum they decided to post into.

The total number of views as at June 2016 was recorded for each post, as was the date of the original date of posting for each post. The latest response to the forum within the January to June 2016 timeframe, and total replies as at time of recording, were also recorded.

Coding

Each forum username (authoring posts or replies actively between January and June 2016) was recorded and allocated a code name. This was to ensure confidentiality and essentially protect user identity. Furthermore, although most RCN usernames seemed quite ambiguous and made it difficult to identify the author, some users assigned their email address as their username, and it was therefore essential that they were each allocated a code name for the study.

3.4.2 Qualitative data

Qualitative data have also been collated and analysed. Thematic analysis was employed to determine the topical information that survey respondents said they had viewed or discussed through online parenting communities. Their rated responses to questions such as, how they perceived the reliability of information ascertained through online social networking, were extended by prompting them to provide further qualitative information to support their ratings. This information is presented within Chapter 4 and Appendices.

3.4.3 Validity

Intercoder reliability was employed to test the validity of the coding and categorisation of the data. Intercoder reliability involves the cross examination of a research method or research tool, employed by a peer researcher (Johnson & Christensen, 2014). This practice determines consistency between coders and is an important indicator of the study's reliability (Johnson & Christensen, 2014). For the purpose of coder reliability, two random samples of the data in this study were generated and issued to two peer coders. Validity of a research instrument can be made when an 80 percent agreement is found amongst coders (Burla et al., 2008).

3.4.4 Intercoder agreement

The first coder independently coded one in every 8 posts analysed, and the second coder independently coded one in every 10 posts analysed. This exercise also assisted with intracoder reliability which concerns identifying coding consistencies within each individual coder (Johnson & Christensen, 2014). The first intercoder was assigned 27 posts to code and the second intercoder coded 21 separate posts. Intercoder 1 agreed with 23 of the 27 codes assigned by the researcher, determining an agreement of 85 percent. The second intercoder agreed with 17 of the 21 codes assigned by the researcher, determining an agreement of 81 percent. This resulted in a mean agreement rate of 83 percent, indicating that high agreement was found between the intercoders.

3.5 Chapter summary

This chapter has outlined the research design and the research methodologies employed in collecting, collating and analysing the data being used to address the two key research questions the research set out to study. A mixed methods research approach was adopted, encompassing a content analysis of a selected period of posts from an online parenting forum, and the analysis of responses to an online survey questionnaire that targeted parents who have utilised social media networks to seek support on matters concerning raising children. An analysis of the main findings emerging from this study is presented in the following chapter.

Chapter 4. Key Findings

This Chapter presents the key findings of this study. These findings are based on data collected in two ways, as explained in Chapter 3. As noted, Stage One comprised of examining online posts on the parenting forums established by the Raising Children Network (RCN), and these findings are presented first. Content analysis was employed to collate and categorise the 210 posts that were active on forums within the RCN website between January and June 2016. The RCN data collated in Stage One make up the first part of the presentation of findings in this Chapter.

In Stage Two, a survey questionnaire on early childhood matters was completed by parents participating in online parenting communities. This survey did not target respondents from any particular social media website, but rather invited respondents who used one or more online media platforms to seek support or information regarding early childhood matters to complete a survey. The findings of this survey are presented in Section 4.3, beginning with a description of the demographic characteristics of the survey respondents. The presentation of the findings in this chapter affirms patterns identified in previous research and reflects new insights on social media use in connection with raising children in Australia today.

4.1   Organisation of the Raising Children Network

The RCN invites individuals raising children to become members of their online forums, where they may seek relevant parenting information and social support. Membership is free of charge; however, all individuals must register, and accept and observe forum interaction guidelines. Moderators approve each user's initial posting before it is uploaded to the site. Subsequent postings are not moderated; however, a disclaimer encourages users to report misuse to the administrator. Apparently dependent upon their frequency of engagement within the forums, members are rated as a *Newbie*, *Junior Member*, or *Supreme Being*. Such status ratings could act as an incentive to increase the sharing of information and provision of social and informational support with community members users.

Deductive inferencing (Krippendorff, 2012) of the data collated found that users of the RCN forums between January and June 2016 were carers of children or were concerned for a child known to them. Analysis of the contents, issues and ideas covered in each posting enabled the identification of a range of common themes reflecting the contents of the posts. Seven categories were established, and each of the 210 posts were assigned to one of the seven categories. The seven categories are identified in Table 1, and further details of posts assigned to each category are tabulated and provided in Appendix A. The information provided in Appendix A includes the title of each post studied together with the user's code name, the number of people who viewed (or read their post), and the number of replies to their post (if any).

When entering the RCN website, it can be seen that it offers four online forums for social interaction, as follows:

1) Baby and Child (n=7)
2) Parents Like Me (n=18)
3) Research (n=2)
4) My Neighbourhood (n=8)

The RCN states that the purpose of these forums is to provide opportunities for families raising children to connect with each other. Each of these four forums comprise a number of sub-forums, as indicated by the numbers identified in the above list. For example, the labels or the titles of the eighteen sub-forums within the 'Parents Like Me' forum (n=18) comprised a range of related topics or issues of relevance to potential participants, as well as the target user characteristics of the RCN website. In this instance, the eighteen sub-forums in the 'parents like me' forum included: mums; dads; expectant dads, Indigenous parents; grandparents and kinship carers; single parents; adoptive and foster parents; step parents; parents of twins and multiples; same-sex parents; parents with depression; special circumstances; parents with fertility issues; pregnancy; parents of children with disability; parents of children with ASD; parents of one-child families; and widows and widowers. It was, however, not possible to verify and confirm the extent to which these forum labels reflected a participant's actual family roles or relationships. The virtual nature of these forums means that it is also not possible to verify whether all participants were indeed living in Australia.

Due to the fragmented organisational nature of the RCN website, the content was collapsed and active data across all RCN forums between January and June 2016 were analysed. As noted, in order to do this, the active posts were searched using the 'latest tab' (see http://tinyurl.com/jgjqj8c), which chronologically presented all posts created and posts that received responses within the study time frame in descending order. Posts uploaded for the purposes of advertising other research, a product or service, during the catchment period of this study, were not included in this analysis. The dates of each post and any reply post were also used to determine their inclusion in this analysis. After scanning the content of these posts, a thematic analysis (Johnson & Christensen, 2014) was conducted to determine commonalities between the topics included in the posts. This analysis enabled the establishment of the 7 categories and led to the allocation of each post to one of the seven categories, as indicated in Table 1. For example, where parents posted questions about local schools, a category for school and education was established, to which such posts were assigned. Table 1 presents a description of the content included in each of the seven categories.

The categorisation of the data through intersubjective interpretations was undertaken by looking at the titles of the posts, which enabled a quantitative analysis of the dialogue within the relevant RCN posts (Krippendorff, 2012). Abductive inferences of the posts were then conducted.

Table 1. Description of categories defined by the content covered by the posts

Category	Description
1. Schooling and Education	This topic reflects user discussions about schooling and education from birth to secondary education.
2. Autism/ABA	This category presents posts by users concerned that their child or their sibling may be autistic, parents whose children were recently diagnosed with autism, or families requesting information about autism, particularly information about Applied Behaviour Analysis (ABA).
3. Challenging Children	User posts about challenging issues such as children's behaviour and difficulties with routine times were assigned to this category. In these posts the user indicated that children's behaviours were interfering with their own well-being and or overall quality of family life. Posts which presented personal conflicts, and conflicts within interpersonal relationships were also placed in this category.
4. Fertility, Pregnancy & Infants	This category represents discussions regarding conception, prenatal concerns and, postnatal issues.
5. Child development and health	Child development and health includes posts which reflect parental concerns for their children's health and development (other than Autism/ABA).
6. Family Matters	The Family matters category represents posts regarding issues with family structure, parent relationships or foster parents. This category also includes messages uploaded by grandparents.
7. Other interests	All posts which reflected topics of interest not covered in the six categories listed above (for example, travel, shopping or babysitting).

4.1.1   Focus topics of postings on RCN

All the posts in the RCN forums included in this study were collated, counted and tabulated as shown in Table 2. All posts analysed in this study are presented together with the number of views and replies for each post, and are available in Appendix A. The number and percentage of posts collated under each topic are reflective of participants' particular interests and engagement in the forum discussions. (Please note that all texts taken from the RCN forums and survey responses are unaltered and may consist of spelling or grammatical errors.)

Table 2. Number of posts collated within each category

Code	Category	No. Posts	Percentage
Topic 1	School and Education	18	9
Topic 2	Autism/ABA*	32	15
Topic 3	Challenging Children	52	26
Topic 4	Fertility, Pregnancy & Infants	25	13
Topic 5	Child development and health	29	14
Topic 6	Family Matters	26	11
Topic 7	Other interests	28	12
	TOTAL	210	100

Figure 3 illustrates the percentage of posts allocated to each topic. This makes it easier to see the overall pattern of postings made according to the seven areas of focus identified.

Figure 3. Topic frequency

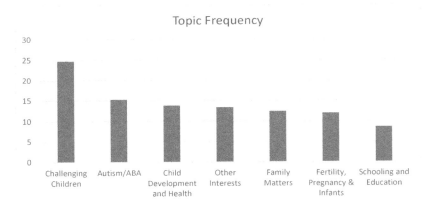

Discussions around Autism accounted for 32 (or 15%) of the 210 posts collated from the catchment period included in this study. This finding is consistent with that of Carlon, Stephenson, and Carter (2015), who found that the majority of families in their study, who had children with autism, found information on the internet and considered this to be somewhat useful. Discussions around Challenging Issues (n=52) made up just over one quarter, or 26% of all posts analysed, making up the biggest proportion of content analysed. Challenging Issues encompassed matters such as chronic bedwetting, tantrums, and upset routine times.

Challenging issues identified by parents with both young children and teenagers were also assigned to this category.

4.2   Online interconnections between RCN community members

This section presents the level or type of interactions and interconnections found amongst the RCN forum members within the forum posts studied. It is hoped that this analysis will provide more insights into the culture of this particular cyber community.

4.2.1 Forum member interactions

User interconnections appear to have been influenced by the topic discussed. Higher levels of support and interaction were found to occur for topics that were less serious or lightweight such as children's activities or baby names. Less interaction and replies were found in posts that were more serious in nature such as child protection or child birth and fertility concerns (please refer to Appendix A for further details such as the number of views and replies to each post studied during the catchment period of this research). A further analysis of the posts indicated that some posts included in the catchment of this research did not receive any replies at all, as indicated in Table 3.

Table 3. Total posts and non-replies for each category

Topic	Total posts	Total non-replies	%
School and Education	18	5	28
Autism/ABA	32	11	34
Challenging Issues	52	11	21
Fertility, Pregnancy & Infants	25	4	16
Child development and health	29	5	17
Family Matters	26	11	42
Other interests	28	16	57

The two most active categories also had the two largest areas of non-replied-to posts: posts referring to Autism and Challenging issues totalled 32 and 52 posts, respectively; and both categories had 11 posts each that were not replied to at all.

The examination of the contents without a reply from anyone reflected a mix of issues/topics/questions that could have benefited from supportive feedback from others, as indicated in the following examples.

RC0382 posted a message about her daughter who had just been diagnosed with autism. She wrote: "4yo girl diagnosed last year, just found this forum!" With her four year old daughter diagnosed with Autism the previous year, this parent was clearly seeking ongoing support. RC0382 would have benefited from some emotional support at this time; but although 676 users read her post at the time, she unfortunately did not receive a single reply.

RC0368 wrote a desperate message entitled: "HELP!! need advice to help get my profoundly deaf son to settle". The dire state of this parent struggling to settle her profoundly deaf son to sleep was apparent; however, RC0368 too failed to receive a reply to her message.

The nature of replies posted also showed that there was typically a time delay when responses appeared throughout the RCN. Sometimes the response did not appear until 12 months or more had passed, as indicated in the following example (please note user posts are provided as is, without corrections to spelling or grammar):

Example 1:
User RC0117 had a nine-month-old child who had just started attending ECE and was experiencing separation anxiety. She wrote a post on March 18, 2013 entitled, 'day care', discussing her daily drop-off routine, and wasn't sure about lingering in the mornings. However, she did not receive a reply to her post until the 22nd of June 2016 by RC0025, who put forward her opinion about parents needing to take care of their babies until they are three years of age. The second reply to her post came on the 27th of June 2016 by RC0092, who simply stated: "Maybe she needs more time. Let her grow one more year and then think of letting her attend the preschool/day care". This conversation thread was viewed by 821 community members.
(See Appendix I, for a full copy of this conversation.)

Not receiving a reply at all was also entirely possible, as reflected in the rate of replies noted in Table 3 and Appendix A.

4.2.2 Helping behaviours

As at the time of analysis, some helping behaviours were found where advice and suggestions were sought and shared amongst forum members. The following correspondence is an example of help being sought and helpful suggestions being offered by forum members:

> Example 1:
> On March 22, 2016, RC0187 wrote about her serious concerns for her daughter who is mixing with troubled children and is also self-harming. She said that her daughter had just been suspended from school. She said that she had arranged to take her daughter to the school counsellor the following day, but her daughter was refusing to go. RC017 was at a loss about what to do, and asked for help and advice through the posting on RCN. On April 3, 2016, RC0188 responded to RC0187, empathising with her circumstances and providing some suggestions and advice.
>
> Although RC0188 provided RC0187 with a detailed and helpful response, it seems that RC0187 did not receive RC0188's response to her original post, as she did not respond to RC0188. This could be attributed to fact that that RC0188 responded nearly 2 weeks after RC0187's post. It must also be noted that RC0187 mentioned that she had an appointment with her daughter's guidance counsellor the following day, so perhaps she was just in need of immediate support from someone that particular evening while waiting for the appointment with the guidance counsellor the next day.
>
> (See Appendix B for a full copy of this conversation.)

This kind of delayed response over two weeks or more was quite typical within the RCN community. The analysis of patterns of responses suggests that, overall, the culture of limited communication within the RCN may be a contributing factor to the low interaction and activity occurring on the RCN forums.

4.2.3 The bystander effect

As discussed in Chapter 2, the bystander effect occurs when more than one person is aware of someone experiencing a potential emergency situation and yet they fail to act (Latané & Nida, 1981). As the number of bystanders increases, the likelihood that someone will render assistance or enact helping behaviours decreases. The bystander effect was found in many of the RCN posts analysed in the present study; and this was found where, although a high number of people viewed a post, few to no replies were offered by online community members. An example of a bystander effect found in the RCN postings is presented as Example 3:

> Example 3:
> In May 2016, RC0155 posted her concerns for her 9-year-old daughter who is dangerously and suddenly absconding from the family home and even from within the car while stopped at traffic lights. Distressed, RC0155 and her and her two younger

children are required to drive around looking for her nine-year-old daughter at all hours of the day or night. Within her post, RC0155 mentioned that her daughter would jump out of the car while she was stopped at traffic lights or run out of the house while she was cooking dinner. In her post, RC0155 mentioned that she is living in a remote community and was unable to readily access support services. "We live in a regional area no Counselling service to hand we have to wait for one to visit the town and the waiting list for an appointment is long" (RC0155).

She asked fellow members of the RCN online community for any advice they might be able to give as they long await professional help to come available. She explains that she is at her wits' end and is very concerned for her daughter's safety. Although over 1,300 RCN users viewed her post, and however dire the situation, RC0155 did not receive one single reply post. Not even from an RCN moderator.

(See Appendix C for full copy of RC0155's post.)

The issue of the low to no response rate on the RCN forums was raised by user RC0130, who posted a blog titled, 'what's the point?' in June 2016. Her post read: "Not to be rude, but I do wonder what the point of this forum is when everyone 'views' your question, but no one responds". This post yielded 712 views at the time; however, that too did not receive a single reply.

4.2.4 Bystander barriers

As noted previously, this study found that many RCN forum participants did not receive many replies to their posts, if at all (see Table 3). Many reply posts in the January to June 2016 catchment period were in response to very old posts, some over six to eight years after the date of the original posting. In fact, 64 (65%) of the 210 active posts within the six-month period did not receive a single reply as at August 2016. This equates to an average 30 percent response rate.

An abundance of replies to other users were found in posts that appeared to be regarding issues to which it was relatively easy to reply, such as a discussion following a post from a user looking for suggestions for baby names: the post title read, "Baby names... Idea's??"; and it yielded 8,100 views and 27 responses of the total data set, accounting for 0.3% of respondent replies. However, bystander barriers were found in posts such as that of RC0046, who was separated from her partner but still living under the same roof. Her post yielded 69,000 views but only received 23 replies. In proportion to the number of views, it is apparent that the user looking for ideas for baby names retrieved an average of one reply for every 300 views, while the person needing advice because she was separated but still living under the same roof as her estranged partner on average yielded only one reply per 3,000 views. This may be due in part to many participants being unable to sympathise with or identify potential implications of her living arrangements. Perhaps many did not know what to say in support. Of the few replies to RC0046 were RCN members who identified with her situation and provided messages of support as they too were in a similar situation. One reply to RC0046 was by a community member who had actually just met someone who was living with her estranged partner and wanted to connect with others in the same situation. However, despite requesting online community members to refrain from any comments of scepticism, she did receive warnings from other RCN community members that her arrangement may not work out.

Furthermore, interests and characteristics of forum users appear to have also played a part in the level of online discussion. For example, posts in the Child Development and Health category yielded 132 replies, the highest number of replies, even though this category experienced only 42,866 views, averaging 142 views per reply. However, the category entitled 'Family Matters', which yielded the most views, totalling 101,888, received only a total of 88 replies, averaging about 1,169 views per reply as at the time of analysis. Table 4 presents the total number of posts, views and replies for each category.

Table 4. Total number of views, posts and replies for each category

Topic	Total views	Total replies	Percentage of replies
School and Education	16152	27	0.17
Autism/ABA	33461	57	0.17
Challenging Issues	86256	162	0.19
Fertility, Pregnancy & Infants	54614	117	0.21
Child development and health	46630	139	0.30
Family Matters	101888	88	0.09
Other interests	21077	24	0.11

A low percentage of replies per post for each category is apparent. It should be noted, however, that due to the nature of the website, it is difficult to identify if or when users choose to connect with other members offline, or set up alternative means of staying connected without going through the RCN forum.

4.3   Findings from the online survey

This section presents findings from Stage Two of the research, comprising the analysis of the online survey responses. The online survey targeted families participating in online communities. The survey was conducted to explore whether or how their participation in social media influenced them in regard to early childhood matters. The online survey consisted of 38 items aimed at ascertaining participants' characteristics and experiences of online social media. There were 91 replies to the survey (including partial responses), and these form the basis of the analysis of findings for Stage Two.

4.3.1 Respondent characteristics

All survey respondents were Australian residents over the age of 18 years who were raising children. In total, there were 91 respondents, and 70 percent of survey respondents completed the survey in its entirety. Thus, the key findings of this survey will refer to the number of responses received for each item.

Sixty-eight percent of respondents said they had children five years of age or younger. All respondents were parents raising children; and only three identified as fathers, while eighty five (97%) were mothers. The majority of Australian states were represented amongst the survey participants, with perecentages of respondents from the various states being: fifty-seven (65%) from New South Wales; eleven respondents (13%) from Queensland; ten respondents from Victoria (11%); seven respondents (8%) from Western Australia; two respondents from the Northern Territory; and one from the Australian Capital Territory. There were no survey respondents from South Australia or Tasmania.

In order to determine the geographical characteristics of parents using online social media, survey respondents were asked about their community type. This data is presented in Figure 4. A large number of respondents (77%) indicated that they lived in city-based metropolitan communities (including one from the Northern Territory). Drentea and Moren-Cross (2005) found that families in urban environments usually have both parents in paid employment, working full time. Full-time employment can isolate parents from their geographical neighbours, and many parents often turned to online social media for networking after hours (Drentea & Moren-Cross, 2005). In the present study, twelve respondents, accounting for 14% of the overall total of participants, were from regional communities (five from regional NSW, four were from regional Queensland, and three from regional Victoria). Of the seven respondents from rural Australia, three were from rural NSW, two were from rural Victoria, one was from rural Queensland, and one was from rural Western Australia.

Figure 4. Community type

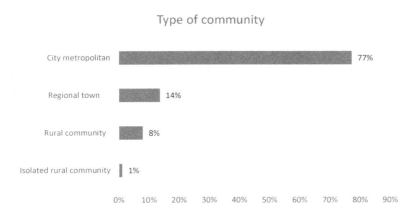

As shown in Figure 5, there were two survey respondents who were between eighteen and twenty years of age (2%). Fifteen respondents were between twenty-one and thirty years of age (17%). Just under half of all respondents were between the ages of thirty-one and forty years (55%); and one quarter of respondents were aged forty-one to fifty years (25%). There was one respondent who identified as a mother from a Metropolitan City area in New South Wales who was fifty-one years or older and was raising children who were all over the age of five years. More than three quarters of the survey respondents were over the age of 30 years. The extent to which they can be perceived as digital immigrants was reflective of the level of comfort in using online technologies.

In order to extend on the work of Drentea and Moren-Cross (2005), survey respondents were asked about their employment status to determine whether their employment status played a part in family use of online social media. Eighty-three percent of respondents (n=73) said they were engaged in paid employment. Over half, or fifty-four percent, of the respondents were employed full time (n=38), seventeen percent were employed for less than 20 hours a week (n=20), and one respondent was employed on a casual or irregular basis.

Figure 5. Respondent age

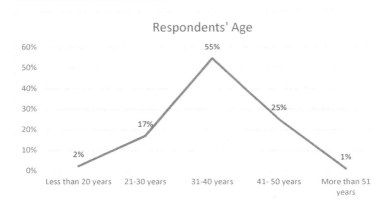

Survey respondents were invited to identify any links to the number of children in each family, the children's ages, and the level of parental use of online social media. There were thirty-five respondents who said they had 1 child (40%), thirty-seven respondents said they had two children (42%), fourteen respondents (16 %) said they had three children, and 2 (2%) respondents said they had four children. As can be seen in Figure 6, the majority of respondents (n=72), accounting for 82 percent, said they had only one or two children.

41

Figure 6. How many children are you currently raising?

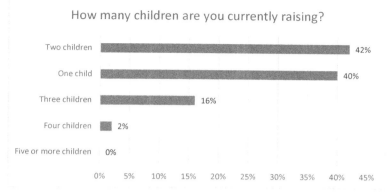

Multiple respondent variables were collated and presented on a graph to provide a snapshot of the survey respondent characteristics including respondent's age, locality, and number of children. This graph shows that most survey respondents (77%) lived in a city metropolitan community, had one to two children, and were predominantly between the ages of thirty-one to forty years. Figure 7 provides a screenshot of survey respondent characteristics, presenting a multivariate analysis of the survey respondents.

Figure 7. Multivariate analysis of survey respondent characteristics

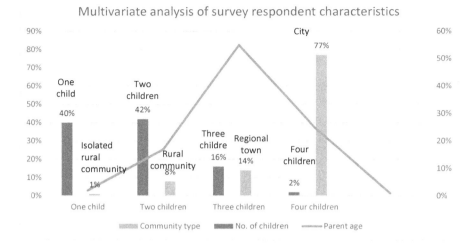

Item number 5 ascertained the ages of the respondent's children. Table 5 presents the ages of the survey respondents' children: children aged between birth and 12 months accounted for 8% (n=10); children aged between 12 months and 2 years accounted for 26% (n=33); children aged between 3 and 4 years of age accounted for 24% (n=30); and children five years of age accounted for 10% (n=13). Thirty-two percent were aged over 5 years (n=41); which leaves close to 70 percent of respondents' children being 5 years of age or under.

Table 5. Ages of survey respondents' children

Age	Percentage	Count
Age between birth to 12 months	8%	10
Age between 1 to 2 years	26%	33
Age 3 to 4 years	24%	30
Aged 5 years	10%	13
Children over 5 years of age	32%	41
Total	100%	127

4.4 Use of ECE services

To further extend the work of Baxter and Hand (2013) survey respondents were asked about the form and frequency of using non-parental services for their children. When asked whether their children had been cared for by anyone other than the parents, eighty-four percent (n=71) of respondents indicated that this had been the case. Fifty respondents (35%) said that they utilised childcare centres for their children; forty-one respondents (29%) said that their children's grandparents cared for their children; and thirteen percent (n=18) indicated the use of a preschool or kindergarten. Eight respondents (6%) said they had used family day care; and twelve respondents (12%) indicated that their children have been cared for by another relative. Eight respondents (6%) indicated the use of a family friend to care for their children; and three (2%) stated that they used a nanny. This data is presented in Figure 8.

Note that, as respondents could choose more than one type of care service, it became apparent that most of the respondents used a combination of options. For example, of the seventy-nine responses to this question, fifty respondents stated that they used each child care arrangement part time; and of these, thirty eight worked full time, Monday to Friday. Therefore, it would be expected that they were using a combination of formal and informal child care arrangements.

Figure 8. Care and education type utilised

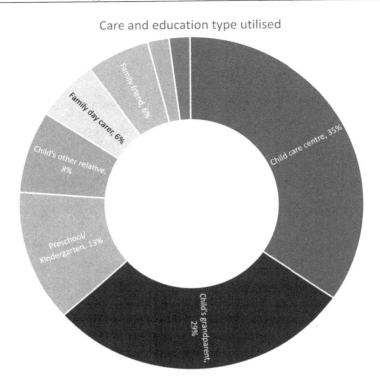

Care and education type utilised

Bowes et al. (2004) found that many families chose to arrange multiple forms of childcare arrangements to enable their children to also regularly spend time with their grandparents, creating a "patchwork" (p. 72) of childcare arrangements. More than ten years later, Grace et al. (2017), writing about this phenomenon, noted this shift in cultural norms within Australian communities. Baxter and Hand (2013) also report finding a high usage rate of grandparents as carers for their grandchildren, in their report for the Australian Institute of Family Studies (AIFS). Furthermore, eleven respondents in the present study said that they used both childcare centres and preschool/kindergarten. This finding is consistent with Baxter and Hand (2013), who found that many families used a combination of different care types at any one time.

In order to ascertain the frequency of care utilisation for each type of care, survey respondents were asked to indicate how regularly they utilised each type of care arrangement. The majority of survey respondents (n=52, or 66%) stated that they used their childcare arrangements on a part-time basis. Of the thirty-eight survey respondents who said they worked full time, five said that their children were not cared for by anyone other than themselves. This could indicate that these respondents worked full time from home while simultaneously caring for their children, or worked in paid employment full time, outside of the nine-to-five business hours, and/or their children were cared for by the other parent who may not have been in paid employment at the same time. Three of the thirty-eight respondents who worked full time said they used a childcare centre for their child on a full time basis. One respondent who worked full time said she used a family friend to care for her child on a full time basis. All five respondents who said that they worked full time but whose children were not cared for by anyone but themselves said they believed ECE was important for their children. This could suggest that the survey respondents were early childhood educators who may feel that they could facilitate their children's ECE at home. These data are presented in Figure 9.

When asked if they used any other type of care, one respondent provided further details, saying that they used a creche, while another respondent said that their child has only ever been cared for by themselves or at school.

Figure 9. How often the child care arrangements were utilised

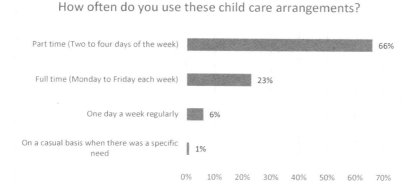

Of the eighty respondents who responded to the question about their beliefs regarding whether every child should attend a formal ECE setting such as a childcare centre or a preschool before starting school, the majority (n=69, or 86%) said yes. The respondents who stated that their children were only cared for by themselves personally also stated that they did believe ECE was beneficial for child development. For example, although acknowledging the developmental benefits that ECE can offer children, survey respondent SR083, a father, also said that he felt he could do a better job by raising his child one-on-one at home. Another respondent, a mother of a three to four year old child, said:

> I believe in ECE and can see the value for a child's development and education. However there are other avenues parents can utilise such as playgroups and Child and Parent Centres to deliver the same opportunities. (SR032)

Another survey respondent who valued home care with a parent stated the following:

> Two of my kids coped well with three year old Kindy but one of mine just hated it and suffered badly with separation anxiety being away from me. It was so traumatising for them to go I ended up pulling him out and just doing Kindy type stuff at home with him, he's 12 now and it certainly didn't affect him education wise. (SR025)

Survey respondent SR065 also believed that parenting information found online may assist parents who were unable to access ECE for their children, in providing educational programs for their own children. She stated:

> Some children whose parents (for many reasons, such as being very busy working, having other important commitments they cannot avoid, low education levels themselves, sickness, disability, relationship breakdown, etc.) are unable to prepare a child for school can access a wide range of educational, social and school readiness experiences that they would otherwise miss out on and it also helps them transition from home to school in terms of daily routine, behavioural expectations such as turn taking, sitting on a mat for group time, etc. and socially. (SR065)

These survey respondent comments indicate that some families believe all ECE outcomes can be achieved in environments other than those in formal ECE settings.

To test the validity of the question regarding respondent perspectives on the importance of ECE, a rating scale was used to further determine the contexts which they found most beneficial for their children's development, as indicated in Figure 10.

Figure 10. Respondent perspectives of ECE

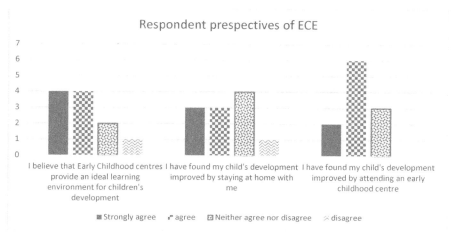

4.5 Information sought by survey respondents online

In order to gauge what information or topics families were exploring through online social media, survey respondents were provided with a range of possible answers, and they could select as many as applicable to them. Information found within the content analysis conducted in Stage One influenced the topical categories identified in these survey questions. For example, the Family Matters category was subdivided into three categories: relationships with a spouse; relationships with immediate family; and relationships with the extended family. This was done in order to gain further insights about the particular interpersonal relationship issues that individuals felt they wanted to discuss within their cyber communities. It was also intended to extend the work of Drentea and Moren-Cross (2005), who have discussed the possibilities of individuals being more likely to share certain intimate issues within their cyber communities than with their family and friends.

Relationships with a spouse accounted for eight percent of total issues discussed. Relationships with immediate family members accounted for five percent of total issues, as did relationships with extended family members. Schools and education accounted for 20 percent of topics discussed, and child development accounted for twenty-four percent, the latter being the greatest percentage of all topics discussed. Anticipating a smaller number of respondents than found on the RCN, child health and Autism were combined for the online survey, keeping the total number of categories down to seven. Children's Health including Autism accounted for eleven percent of topics discused online by survey respondents.

Participants were also provided with the opportunity to add further information regarding other topics they may have read about online that were not already listed. Consistencies were found between topics explored by families on the RCN and those of the survey respondents, as presented in Figure 11.

Figure 11. Type of posts survey respondents have been looking at online

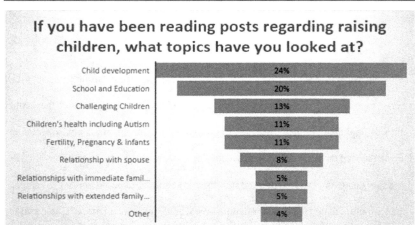

Four percent of survey respondents (n= 4) provided further information about topics that they had discussed on social media (that were not already prelisted), and these included:

- Safety first aid (SR083)

- Play, Natural Play, Homeschooling, Nutrition, Art, Maggie Dent; (SR081)

- Eating solids (SR058)

- Breast feeding, La Leche League and ABA (SR051)

- Social development (SR047)

- Stimulating and fun activities to do with toddlers (SR021)

- Health issues (SR020)

- Eating habits (SR018)

Respondents also noted that they had posted questions on social media about topics such as: Children's Health and Development; child safety/first aid; education and parent teacher communication; additional needs; toilet training; pregnancy, babies and breastfeeding; routine times; spousal separation; networking; and recreational activities for children.

4.6 Interconnections established through blogs compared to social status updates

McDaniel et al. (2012) found differing levels of connectedness and relatability occurring between online blog community members who read, write and respond to online blogs, compared to that between individuals engaging in online social networking in the form of uploading and reading social status updates.

In order to extend this research, survey respondents in the present study were asked whether they experienced a greater sense of connectedness by reading or publishing online blogs, or by publishing and reading status updates made on social media networking sites. It was found that survey respondents experienced equal levels of connectedness, by reading blogs (37.4%), and by reading status updates on social media sites (37.4%). Lower levels of connectedness were found for respondents when publishing both status updates (41.6%) and/or blogs (17%). These findings were consistent with those of the experiences of forum members within the RCN. That is, users of social media appeared to be reading online social networking material more than they were responding to online social networking material. These data are presented as a bar graph in Figure 12.

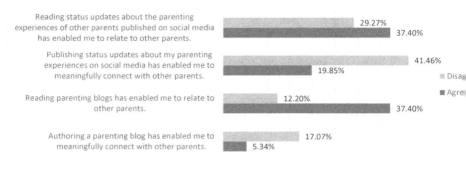

Bivariate analysis contrasting levels of connectedness found by blogging to that of social networking

As shown in Figure 12, the majority of survey respondents (41%) did not agree that publishing status updates on social media had enabled them to connect with other parents. Instead the analysis showed that reading parenting blogs and reading status updates about other parents' experiences were helpful in relating to others participating in online social networks. This pattern is consistent with the findings of McDaniel et al. (2012) who found a higher level of connectedness for participants by reading parenting blogs.

4.7 Cyber lurking

Reading posts and failing to reply to posts constitutes cyber lurking. Paterson, Brewer, and Stamler (2013) found 50-90% of cyber community members to be cyberlurkers. To further identify cyber lurking behaviour patterns found in Stage One of this study and in previous research presented in the literature review in Chapter 2, survey respondents were also asked about their online social networking interactions.

When asked whether they have ever responded to someone's post online, only 52 percent of respondents said they had replied. These findings are consistent with the literature reviewed and with the community member interactions found within Stage 1 of this study. One example of cyber lurking was provided by a survey respondent (SR056) who simply said that it is good to know that other people were concerned or experiencing the same things they were. This could indicate that SR056 was satisfied with just reading what other people wrote online and could relate to others without directly engaging in an online dialogue.

When asked to provide details regarding why they had not responded to someone's blog or post online, twenty-eight survey respondents offered a range of explanations, as follows:

- I avoid engaging in comments - too controversial. (SR062)
- Just like to observe. (SR052)
- Don't like to post comments on social media. (SR029)
- I don't like that my reply can be seen by anyone. If it was private I might reply. (SR017)

(See Appendix D for the full list pertaining to respondent reasoning for not replying to posts online.)

4.8 Online social media experiences

When asked whether their child's or family's experiences had been influenced by information gained through online social networking, fifty-seven percent of respondents (n= 39) said 'a little', 16% (n= 11) said 'moderately', and 7 percent (n=5) said 'totally'. This indicates that 80 percent of survey respondents felt that their experiences on social media had influenced their lives and that of their children to some degree. Almost half, or fifty-four percent, of respondents said that they found the advice of other parents online more useful than advice they had received from healthcare professionals. This data is presented in Figure 13. Specific examples of survey respondent feedback regarding their social networking experiences include:

- Having a response from another mother/father is better knowledge than I can find through a book for instance. Real life reviews from other parents advising their techniques that have assisted them through any issues. I have used multiple difference responses and used what I felt was best for our situation. (SR018)
- Whenever I am faced with a parenting issue I don't know how to approach, I will go online to see what information I can find, either through groups I'm a part of, or by looking up blogs. (SR072)

These comments are consistent with the work of Sarkadi and Bremberg (2005), who found that parents appreciated parenting advice that derived from the practical experiences of other parents in contrast to getting expert advice from others including health professionals.

Figure 13. Survey respondent perspectives of online advice

I found the online advice I received from other parents more useful than the advice I received from health professionals

Social media experiences, as an influence on the lives of children and families, were also examined in the survey. For this item, fifty-five of the sixty-nine survey respondents indicated that they felt their social media experiences had influenced the experiences of their children and their families to some degree. This data is presented in Figure 14. When asked to provide more information in regard to how, respondents' comments included examples such as the following:

> [Social networking] gave me the confidence to follow my instincts in a lot of areas such as sleeping, starting school, getting my daughter assessed for ASD. Given me lots and lots of ideas of activities for weekends and school holidays. Helped me understand information that professionals tend to over complicate. (SR065)
> Having a response from another mother/father is better knowledge than I can find through a book for instance. Real life reviews from other parents advising their techniques that have assisted them through any issues. I have used multiple difference responses and used what I felt was best for our situation. (SR018)

Conversely, another respondent said:

> I appreciate the opportunity to connect with other parents (on social media) however I find there is a lot of information on social media sites that's pseudo-scientific, lacks empirical evidence and is often based on personal experience. Personal experience

counts for a lot but needs to be weighted against empirical evidence. I have seen plenty of mums in my circle of friends who have 'fallen for the preachings of a self-proclaimed parenting expert'. (SR057)

Figure 14. Social media influences on family and child experiences

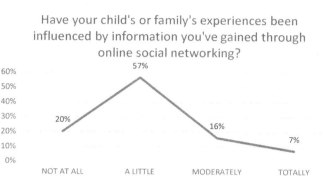

Have your child's or family's experiences been influenced by information you've gained through online social networking?

When asked whether social media has changed their views in regard to parenting and ECE, the majority of survey respondents (n=80) indicated that it did so to some extent. This data is presented in Figure 15. When asked if they could provide further information to elaborate on this, SR066 said that it "somewhat changed my mind on certain things"; and SR034 said, "Worrying about what others think has affected some decisions".

Figure 15. Social media influences on parenting and ECE

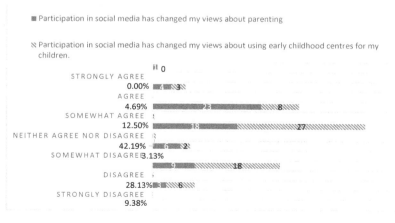

■ Participation in social media has changed my views about parenting

▧ Participation in social media has changed my views about using early childhood centres for my children.

STRONGLY AGREE
0.00%

AGREE
4.69%

SOMEWHAT AGREE
12.50%

NEITHER AGREE NOR DISAGREE
42.19%

SOMEWHAT DISAGREE
3.13%

DISAGREE
28.13%

STRONGLY DISAGREE
9.38%

54

When survey respondents were provided with the opportunity to indicate how they have benefited from using socia media, twenty percent said that social networking provided them with new information, sixteen percent said that it made them feel better knowing that they are not alone as a parent, ten percent said that social media linked them with education services for their child, and thirteen percent said that social media helped them to network with other parents in similar circumstances. This information is presented in Figure 16.

Figure 16. How parents have benefited from online social networking

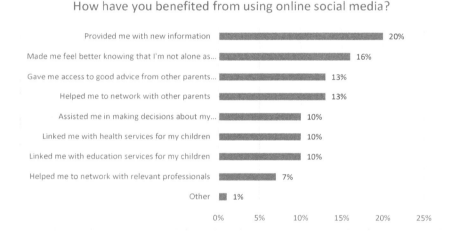

Respondents who provided further details about how social networking supported them made comments such as the following:

- Learn new skills, connect with people with similar interests, ideas for interaction and play to do with the children. (SR081)
- Social media helped me connect with and stay connected with people (particularly other mums) during the early stages of motherhood. (SR072)
- Gave me fresh ideas, reassured me I was not alone, made me feel less isolated as a single mum, pointed me in the direction of services, professionals and attractions. (SR065)
- I became an administrator on an online parenting group, to support other breastfeeding mums with questions and connecting with other likeminded

mums - I took this role on as a result of how much the online community helped me in my early mothering journey (SR072).

Furthermore, sixty-nine survey respondents provided information regarding their perspectives on the effectiveness of social media in regard to gaining information in relation to raising children. Their responses resulted in a mean of 48.97, standard deviation of 25.06, and variance of 628.06. This information is presented as a histogram in Figure 17.

Figure 17. Effectiveness of social media in relation to gaining information about raising children

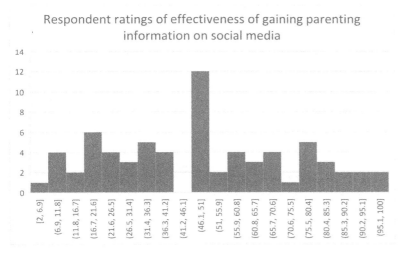

In regard to the extent to which survey respondents felt that social media networking enabled them to connect with other parents, sixty-nine respondents provided percentages resulting in a mean score of 54.7, standard deviation of 28.17 and variance of 793.53. To determine the correlation between community type and survey respondent perspectives regarding the effectiveness of social media in connecting with other parents, a slider scale was provided allowing each respondent to choose a rating from 0 to 100. Their responses were collated and a bivariate analyis was conducted; and the results are presented as a box plot in Figure 18. The results indicate that individuals from regional towns have found social media to be more effective in connecting with other families, more so than for respondents from city/metropolitan communities. The lower ratings provided by respondents from rural communities and isolated rural communities could be due in part to a less reliable internet connection being available within such communities.

Figure 18. Boxplot of social media effectiveness in connecting with other parents

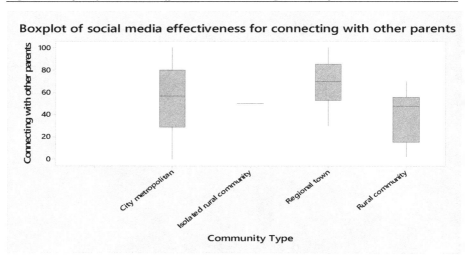

4.9 Extending online friendships and interactions into the 'real' world

Many survey respondents reported making offline contact with other parents whom they met online. In fact, of the 79 respondents who answered this question, 38 (48%) stated that they had made offline contact with people they had met online. Almost one quarter of the survey respondents (23%, or n=18) stated that they had met in person; ten percent (n=8) made contact by text message, seven percent (n=6) stated they made contact through other social media; four percent (n=3) spoke on the phone; and four percent (n=3) had made contact through personal email. These data are presented as a bar graph in Figure 19.

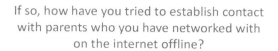

If so, how have you tried to establish contact
with parents who you have networked with
on the internet offline?

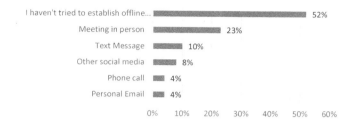

When asked about how confident they felt about the reliability of social media to obtain information about parenting matters, 69 respondents answered, providing a mean of 46.1 and standard deviation of 26.2. The data are presented as a histogram in Figure 20, providing an indication of variation between respondent perspectives on the reliability of social media to obtain parenting information.

Figure 20. Respondent confidence in social media as a reliable source for parenting information

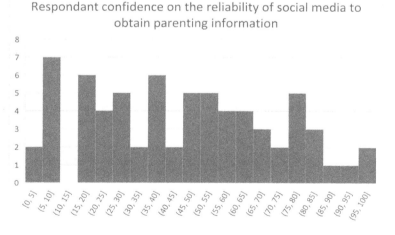

Respondant confidence on the reliability of social media to obtain parenting information

In reference to whether they would recommend social media to other parents, almost three quarters of survey respondents (73%) said 'yes'. In regard to her perspective on the reliability of some of the information gained through social media platforms, survey respondent

58

SR055 said it's "not research based or necessarily best practice". However, many survey respondents reported using social media for social support: for example, survey respondent SR059 said:

> "There are some helpful apps/forums such as BabyCentre that have helpful information. Connecting with some accounts on Instagram also provide healthy positive thoughts".

Survey respondent SR026 said:

> "In the right places, it can feel a bit like "a village". Especially when kids are very young. Feel less isolated that way".

SR075, who would not recommend social networking to peers, said: "I think social media can be positive for some, but I also think it can be very negative. Humans will naturally compare and I don't think that is good for families". SR078 said: "I would recommend it but to recognise that just as in the 'real' world there are many different opinions with regards to raising children. In the Mums group I connect with, vaccinations and circumcisions are banned topics".

4.10 Chapter summary

This chapter presented the key findings of this study. There were no major differences found between online blogs and social networking sites in the way participants interacted within online communities. The majority of participants reported that online platforms and social media interactions have influenced the experiences of their families and children to some limited extent, whilst a strong twenty percent claimed that it has had no impact at all. Cyber lurking behaviours were identified in both the RCN forum activity and by survey respondents. There were common themes about information being sought online, across the content of online data analysed from the RCN and the topics indicated by the survey respondents. The majority of the survey respondents also indicated that belonging to an online community reduced their sense of isolation and provided them with a place where they gained information and emotional support. It was found that respondents appreciated the advice received through social media more so than the information they received from health professionals. A discussion of these findings takes place in the following Chapter.

Chapter 5: Discussion

This chapter presents a reflective discussion of the main findings of this study mapped against the two key research questions it set out to investigate. The first section provides an overview of the context of the study, which is then followed by a summary of the key findings, which are aligned with the research questions. Implications for policy, practice and suggestions for further research are also provided for each key finding. A summary of parental perspectives on ECE found throughout the course of this study is also provided.

5.1 Contextualising the study

With the majority of survey respondents being mothers (97%), it would appear that traditional gender roles and responsibilities regarding children's health and development issues continue to prevail (Sarkadi & Bremberg, 2005). This finding is quite surprising, considering that the digital arena has been found to be predominantly socially unbiased (Sarkadi & Bremberg, 2005). However, the Sarkadi and Bremberg study was conducted in Sweden over ten years ago, and may not be applicable to today's Australian society. Importantly, the anonymity afforded to participants of social media networks means that it is difficult to verify or authenticate the demographic characteristics of individuals such as those who participated in the RCN forums.

5.2 Key findings

This section provides a summary of the key findings mapped against the research questions underpinning this study. Consistencies found between the literature reviewed in Chapter 2 and the findings made in the course of this study are presented.

Table 6. Summary of research questions and key findings

RQ1: What topics or issues are reflected in Australian parents' online interactions regarding early childhood matters?	
Key finding #1:	Parents who are experiencing adversity such as challenging issues, difficult children, or interpersonal relationship breakdown, are more inclined to turn to social media networking for information and support.
RQ2: How has participation in social media influenced parents about early childhood matters?	
Key finding #2:	Social media networks have influenced parental thinking about raising children to some extent.
Key finding #3:	Parents reported that social media use has assisted them in connecting with other parents.
Key finding #4:	The majority of parents who completed the online survey reported that they had not replied to someone's post online.
Key finding #5:	Parents participating in the online survey valued the experiences of their online peers more so than expert advice provided by health professionals

Each of these findings are discussed next, together with a consideration of

implications for policy and practice, and suggestions for future research.

RQ1: What topics or issues are reflected in Australian parents' online interactions regarding early childhood matters?	
Key finding #1:	Parents who are experiencing adversity such as challenging issues, difficult children, or interpersonal relationship breakdown, are more inclined to turn to social media networking for information and support.

In line with Drentea and Moren-Cross (2005), many families in the present study were

found to address issues within online social networks that they seemingly could not discuss in

person with family and friends for a variety of reasons, or for which they required a second

opinion. Issues found within the RCN forum content, such as challenging children, marital

separation, and relationship issues with immediate and extended family members, were

predominantly the topics discussed online. This could also be attributed to parents needing a

second opinion on advice or support that they may have received from others in real life. Issues

relating to family matters were also investigated further through the survey. In order to ascertain

more specific information regarding interpersonal relationships, this topic was segmented into

3 parts: relationships with spouse, relationships with immediate family members, and

relationships with extended family members. This provided a better indication of what individuals were experiencing in terms of their relationships with a spouse and/or their spouses' family of origin, and which influenced them in turning to online social media to vent, ask for advice, or seek emotional support.

Implications for policy, practice and suggestions for further research.

As discussed, findings of this research show that many parents were turning to online social media networking for advice on challenging or difficult interpersonal issues connected with raising children. In order to ensure that parental needs for social and emotional support are met efficiently and appropriately, moderators of online parenting forums can incorporate a guaranteed response policy that could encourage community members to post a response, for instance through the creative use of pop-up windows with flashing lights. Specifically, online community members need to be made aware that their personal experiences in a similar situation can assist others, and that professional knowledge and expertise is not always required to be of help to someone. Further research into why individuals trust the advice of peers who have been in a similar situation to that of advice offered by professional practitioners may assist in strengthening the confidence of online community members in offering advice and support in regard to challenging interpersonal issues.

Moderator interventions are further recommended in providing research-based information when only traditional values are reinforced by community members, as found in the 'day care' discussion thread. It is imperative that references to quality practice based on research evidence are offered in a timely and informative way. It is evident that many members of online communities are reading posts that may be relevant to their situation without replying to them. Appropriate moderator interventions would ensure all those viewing the thread can also make an informed decision as well as offer support to others in the network.

RQ2:	How has participation in social media influenced parents about early childhood matters?
Key finding #2:	Social media networks have influenced parental thinking about raising children to some extent.

This finding is quite considerable in demonstrating the potential influence online networks can offer in terms of advice and support for individuals raising children. Also emphasised is the vulnerability imposed upon individuals due to the potential anonymity and invisibility afforded on the internet, and thereby indirectly influencing the approaches certain members may take when responding to someone online. The importance of positive and supportive communication channels used by community members is paramount, in particular when networking online with individuals who can be significantly isolated and experiencing any associated emotional effects or mental health issues.

Implications for policy, practice and suggestions for further research.

Social responsibilities of members within online communities (Anker & Feeley, 2011) must be made clear and upheld. Such online responsibilities may encompass: avoiding making comparisons with or between online peers (Coyne, McDaniel, & Stockdale, 2017); refraining from making judgmental comments or belittling fellow peers; or simply providing some empathetic support or referral to a relevant community service. Online social responsibilities need to be incorporated within website interaction policies and guidelines. Furthermore, moderators of online forums may wish to consider monitoring online interactions and applying sanctions on any breeches of ethical conduct online. Research into individual parents who are no longer using online platforms for social support may be warranted, in order to identify the type of information or experiences that may have led them to no longer seek support or information from other parents online.

RQ2:	How has participation in social media influenced parents about early childhood matters?
Key finding #3:	Parents reported that social media use has assisted them in connecting with other parents.

This finding was examined in two separate items within the online survey. Item number 16 asked respondents how they felt they had benefited from using online social media. Respondents reported 'networking with other parents' as one benefit, which made up for thirteen percent of parent responses. 'Gaining access to advice from other parents in similar circumstances' also made up for thirteen percent of parent responses. This finding emphasises the phenomenon that social media networking is, to some degree, replacing traditional face-to-face social interactions and information-seeking procedures. Item number 33 sought to find whether survey respondents had ever made any attempts to seek offline contact with parents they had met online. Almost half, or forty-eight percent, of survey respondents reported making some form of contact with other parents they had met online. This finding redefines interactions that occurred within traditional communities and networking methods once defined by geography and/or life stage, in particular mother's groups or play groups.

Implications for policy, practice and suggestions for further research.

This finding may assist ECE services and healthcare clinics to encourage parents who are unable to physically attend mothers'/fathers' groups or playgroups to join online support groups characterised as having other members in similar circumstances. A newborn's routine in the first year of life can significantly isolate new mothers (McDaniel et al., 2012). Furthermore, complications such as premature birth, birth by caesarean section, or newborns with health issues, can also physically isolate new families. Thus, hospitals, nurses, maternity wards and or midwives may wish to consider promoting online parenting networks as support groups to families, as a routine or regular recommendation. Further research into the experiences of online social networking by these families can expand our knowledge and understanding of the experiences of families isolated in the very early stages following child birth.

RQ2:	How has participation in social media influenced parents about early childhood matters?
Key finding #4:	Majority of parents who completed the online survey reported that they had not replied to someone's post online.

This finding is consistent with the work of Paterson, Brewer, and Stamler (2013), who found that up to fifty percent of online users engaged in cyber lurking behaviours. Support for this finding was found in the present study, where over forty-one percent of survey respondents said they had never posted a note on social media. The low level of online support and absence of reciprocal interactions were clearly evident in the RCN forums, with 30 percent of the total posts studied not receiving a single reply.

Social and emotional support offered through social networks can enrich health and well-being (Bambina, 2007). Online support networks are free of geographic, demographic and time constraints in offering the benefits of social support traditionally offered physically or through direct contact with another person (Bambina, 2007). The level of informational support provided on the RCN during the catchment period of the present research was exemplary. This website provided a plethora of research-based information regarding child development and health, relevant to families with children from birth to adolescence. However, analysis of the RCN forum content suggests that user compulsion to provide or extend social and emotional support online remained at an embryonic stage for a large proportion of the online community members. Although there was protection afforded by the anonymity of the internet, lack of awareness of their own social responsibility meant that many RCN participants enacted digital bystander behaviour as they were left to their own devices to overcome virtual barriers.

Implications for policy, practice and suggestions for further research.

Members within online parenting communities need to be made aware of their social obligation to render assistance when they have identified that a peer is in need of advice and/or support. However, moderators could also effectively respond to posts that do not receive any replies within a certain timeframe such as one month. The time allocated may also vary depending on the seriousness and urgency of the issue identified in each post. Further research into the various ways in which online community members can be encouraged to engage in online discussions will assist to broaden tools and strategies that may increase the social capital that can be offered within online social media platforms. Such studies may also engage in investigating whether online community members are having their emotional and informational needs met by simply reading posts.

RQ2: How has participation in social media influenced parents about early childhood matters?	
Key finding #5:	Parents participating in the online survey valued the experiences of their online peers more so than expert advice provided by health professionals

Consistent with the work of Sarkadi and Bremberg (2005), the present study also found that most parents valued the personal experiences of other parents over the expert advice of health professionals. This finding suggests that parents can feel free to use their own personal experiences as a source of information for other parents, rather than feeling inhibited from replying to someone's questions for fear of giving the wrong answer.

Implications for policy, practice and suggestions for further research

It is recommended that moderators and website developers of parenting websites encourage their online community members to share their own experiences with their online peers. By incorporating guidelines that would encourage helping behaviours into their online social networking policies, the level of informational, emotional and social support that can be gained through online parenting websites could be better facilitated.

5.3 Parents' perspectives on ECE

In their research, Baxter and Hand (2013) found that employed families were more likely to access ECE for their children. This is consistent with the finding in the present study, where of the 73 respondents who were in paid employment, 60 accessed ECE for their children in the form of child care, preschool or a combination of both. Of the fifteen survey respondents who were not in paid employment, nine still believed that children should attend some form of ECE prior to starting school. This finding is also consistent with Coley et al. (2013), who found that Australian families who are aware of the benefits of ECE for their children were more likely to utilise ECE regardless of their employment status. Only four respondents who did not work, did not utilise preschool services nor believed that all children should attend some form of ECE prior to starting school.

Content analysis of relevant online data examined in this study did not incorporate information depicting parent perspectives about the benefits of formal ECE services. Three of the twenty-seven posts within this category identified 'day care', 'fear of going to childcare' and 'when to start school'. The first two posts were based on separation difficulties. Discussions within the third post, regarding 'when to start school', did not refer to use of ECE services but to the predicament of when to send a child to school. This may be an indication that such families with young children were mostly seeking online support when experiencing a dilemma or emotional issues such as separation anxiety experienced when attending an ECE service for the first time.

Baxter and Hand (2013) note that participation in ECE is often based on parents' beliefs about non-parental care or the availability of a parent to care for their children at home. Thus, seeking support or reassurance regarding when to send a child to school, or whether or not to continue to utilise childcare (particularly where a child is experiencing separation anxiety), may be indications that there was a parent who was available to care for the children, and that therefore they could consider non-parental care and education options.

This pattern of variable care options is also consistent with comments made by survey respondents in this research. Although all survey respondents who answered this question indicated their positive perspectives regarding the benefits of ECE, ten participants said that they did not believe that all children should access ECE settings prior to starting school. Reasons for this include issues with affordability and separation anxiety. The majority of survey respondents stated that they believed that some parents may prefer to care for and educate their children at home as opposed to using non-parental care and education. Certain survey respondents suggested that parents can substitute for non-parental ECE. These findings also indicate that some families were not aware of the interpersonal and intrapersonal skills children can develop by interacting with peers in formal ECE settings (Denham, Bassett, & Zinsser, 2012). However, most survey respondents did indicate their perspective that ECE was essential for their children's socialisation, school readiness, immunity against various childhood illnesses, and language and emotional development. For example, survey respondent SR026 said, "I don't think any parent can expose their child enough to social situations with other kids the same age group"; and survey respondent SR059 said: "The social learning play-based experiences are so valuable to the child as they construct knowledge. I believe this cannot be replicated at home with parents or grandparents, if the child is alone".

5.4 Chapter summary

This chapter presented the key findings of this study, which aligned with the research questions underpinning this investigation. The discussion provided an analysis of social media use found within the realm and context of this study, and provided implications for policy and practice, and suggestions for further research. Effectively, social networking experiences have been shown to influence family perspectives and decision making, which consequently impact on children's experiences and child development. The next Chapter synthesises the key learnings that have been derived from this study, and concludes the thesis.

Chapter 6: Conclusions

This study examined the nature of online social networking amongst parents residing in Australia and their perceptions about how their interactions on social media networks have influenced raising children matters. It focused on understanding the information being sought and satisfaction with what was attained, in order to consider implications and recommendations for improved online policies, and interactive tools and facilities available within online community forums. These insights can contribute to better equipping community members for responding to the posts of their online peers on social networking sites focused on raising children matters.

6.1 Key learnings from the study

Analysis of communications within the RCN forums provided insights into the topics of interest and areas in raising children that are concerning parents. Furthermore, the analysis conducted in Stage One provided insights into the aspects of online social networks that have facilitated the online community culture and potentially influenced the parenting of children of the social media network members. Based on the findings of the online survey questionnaire used in Stage Two, key findings about the actual experiences of parents who have participated in social media networking were then discussed, highlighting new insights about the benefits of social media and its impact on raising children today.

6.1.1 Parenting Information sought online

In this study, topics and information families seek online were reviewed, firstly, by reviewing content on a parenting website, and secondly by inviting online survey respondents who participated on online parenting communities to share their experiences regarding social media networking. Content and thematic analysis of this data found that challenging issues were the focus of the majority of postings on the RCN forums. That is, postings about 'challenging issues' accounted for twenty-six percent of all online activity between January and June 2016.

However, survey respondents predominantly reported turning to social media networking for issues regarding 'child development', and these reports represented almost one quarter (24%) of all total topics selected. This suggests that there will be variation in the topics of interest between and across social media networks, and that further research is needed to develop insights about trends over time and to analyse factors contributing to these trends. Survey respondents provided insights into why they turn to online social media support, such as for 'getting advice' or 'ideas' or to be able to relate to others and know that they are not alone. This is consistent with McDaniel et al. (2012), who found that online activity provided isolated parents with a distraction and a sense "that they are not alone" (p. 1510).

The low level of replies to each post found in this study could be, in part, due to the number of views each post received. It is, therefore, hypothesised that families could be turning to online forums when feeling as though they are alone but that, when they read posts written by someone who is experiencing the same issue, their need to relate to others may have been met by simply reading a post that mirrored their own situation. This, in itself, may be the reason why certain online participants did not feel compelled to reply. For example, two of the survey respondents, who provided further information as to why they have never replied to someone's blog or post online, simply said they "did not feel the need" (SR038) and had "not felt it necessary" (SR010). However, this hypothesis needs further testing, to clarify these patterns of online behaviour in order to understand the possibilities of cyber lurking (Paterson et al., 2013).

6.1.2 Electronic communication and online community cultures

A range of electronic communication cultures were observed both within the online RCN forums and in those perspectives shared by survey respondents which ranged from passive online support to extension of social interactions and relationships within the physical world.

6.1.3 Digital bystander barriers

Bystander barriers, as defined by Burn (2009), comprise: i) failure to notice; ii) failure to identify situation as high risk; iii) failure to take intervention responsibly; iv) failure to intervene due to skills deficit; and v) failure to intervene due to audience inhibition (p. 3). According to Scaffidi Abbate, Boca, Spadaro, and Romano (2014), these barriers can inhibit user interactions and helping behaviours. It is imperative that social actors are informed in noticing and identifying that someone is in need of help, and take reasonable responsibility and action to intervene. In simply having been made aware of the bystander effect, individuals may be enabled to overcome this effect.

Digital bystander barriers (Latané & Nida, 1981) may have occurred in instances where forum participant issues seemed quite complex and perhaps may have warranted professional intervention. With most online community members being other lay parents raising children, complexities of their situations could have posed barriers to members identifying a peer in need, accepting responsibility to assist, and in turn enacting helping behaviours (Anker & Feeley, 2011). This reflects what Anker and Feeley have described as "pluralistic ignorance" (p. 14). Moderators of online parenting websites may wish to empower online community members to simply provide their peers some form of sympathy and or referral to professional services, in the event that they feel unqualified to provide specific advice or suggestions to a complex issue or post.

6.1.4 Cyber lurking

Analysis of posts on the Raising Children Network (RCN) has found cyber lurking behaviours within the online community. Users of the RCN were also privy to the number of views of each post. That is, whenever a user opens and reads a post, the view is added to a tally under the column entitled 'views'. In this case, RCN users can experience the implicit bystander effect when they see a large amount of online traffic occurring and imagine that someone else will surely and eventually reply to the post. Latané and Darley (1970) described this as the multiple onlooker effect. Patterson et al. (2013) estimated that over fifty percent of online community members are cyber lurkers. Cyber lurkers predominantly read posts but fail to engage in online interactions with their cyber community members. As mentioned in previous sections in this Chapter, cyber lurking behaviours could be a result of various reasons, including:

- Experiencing a sense of connectedness or relatability with online peers after simply reading posts that mirror one's own circumstances;
- Engaging in online social media forums solely for the unintended entertainment value (Pedersen & Smithson, 2010);
- Bystander barriers restricting enactment of prosocial behaviours (Anker & Feeley, 2011).

6.1.5 Passive support

Passive support was often provided in lieu of criticism (Drentea & Moren-Cross, 2005) resulting in bystander inactivity (Anker & Feeley, 2011). For example, when RCN members asked for advice, respondents provided some feedback or expressed caution indirectly rather than giving direct advice or criticism. Survey respondents provided candid examples of giving passive support, such as SR062, who said: "I avoid engaging in comments - too controversial." This comment provides social media website moderators with a critical example of the passive support behaviours that are occurring on the sites they have established as supportive forums. Findings of the present study reinforce the importance of online community members needing guidance and assistance to identify situations that they could contribute to, and to overcome inhibitions about taking social risks to intervene and enact prosocial behaviours. In relation to utilising social media, one survey respondent stated: "Good to know other people are concerned about the same things" (SR056). This is an indication that this respondent passively utilised social media simply by being aware of others posting on the forum who were experiencing the same issues or concerns.

6.1.6 Parental satisfaction with online information, interaction and support

Parents with young children can often feel isolated from other families, and electronic-based communication can assist families to gain support and information from peers (Hall & Irvine, 2009). Paterson, Brewer, and Stamler (2013) found that parents need to connect with and relate to other parents. However, content analysis of the forum activity within the RCN network in the present study found a high level of dissatisfaction regarding the level of support attained from forum members. As mentioned in the findings Chapter, one RCN member (RC0130) said that she did not see the point of writing posts which everyone viewed but to which no one replied. Pedersen and Smithson (2010) found that ninety-one percent of respondents indicated that they found the content on their topic of interest present in a parenting website entertaining and fun to read (contrary to the stated purpose of online social media communities). Anker and Feeley (2011) suggest that many members of online forums were unaware of their social responsibility to provide support to peers when participating in online community forums. This lack of awareness conflicts with popular views that cyber communities are spaces where members can readily attain information and support from their peers. Furthermore, if one assumes that, by its very nature, social support is reciprocal, this then means that one who is seeking support would naturally expect to receive a response.

Of the forty-four survey respondents who said they had posted a note on social media, two said that they did not receive a response. When asked how they felt about not receiving a reply to the post, both respondents did not comment. As Hudson and Bruckman (2009) suggest, "for a speaker to speak there must be an audience; for a discussion to continue, the audience must respond" (p. 165). Therefore, without a response, a discussion cannot be participated in or exist.

It is apparent from this study, that some online interactions have influenced family decision making and ultimately the experiences of their children. This was evident through a number of survey respondents who provided examples of how their experiences on social media have influenced their children's learning and development. For example, SR081 said that social media helped her to "learn new skills, connect me with people with similar interests, ideas for interaction and play to do with my kids"; and SR072 said: "Social media helped me connect with, and stay connected with people (particularly other mums) during the early stages of motherhood". These comments validate the usefulness of the social ecology approach as a framework for describing how family social and informational supports available within the exosystem can impact children's lives, learning and development (Bowes, Grace, & Hayes, 2012).

6.2 Conceptual model for online collaboration

Raising children matters is just one of many topics that are used as the focus point for online discussions. The conceptual model for online collaboration is presented in the Nabla (inverted triangle), shown in Figure 21. This model illustrates a system in which online content, interactions and online features can trigger a bystander effect in the absence of proper guidelines and policies informing cyber communities of their social responsibilities online. Parental wellbeing, informed decision making, and children's experiences impacting on child development, are vulnerable to the levels of support offered to parents. One of the strengths of this model is its wider application to other contexts.

Figure 21. Model for online collaboration

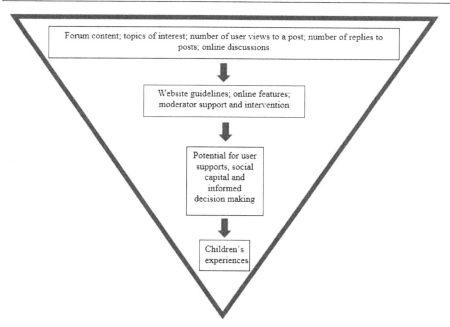

This model is an outcome of the findings of the present study, and contributes to advancing knowledge in the EC sector where the importance of collaboration between educators and families is well recognised. This model can assist both moderators and participants of social media networks to understand the impact of participation through online postings, and how they can contribute to better supporting parents with children through these networks. It has the potential to strengthen collaboration between the various stakeholders; and this is important in today's complex society, which can benefit from better access to supportive networks.

6.3 Limitations and strengths of the present study

The generalisability of the findings in the present study may be made with broader research into online cultures and user interactions across multiple Australian Parenting website forums. Social practices, policies and procedures facilitating informational, social and emotional support within a range of cyber communities will support discoveries that can lead to change and improvements in the way online participants interact and assist fellow community members. Furthermore, attracting a greater number of survey respondents which equally represent each state and territory will offer a greater perspective on and better represent national trends in online support community interactions.

This study has extended Australian literature and research in the area of social media networking for parents. The findings can be used to optimise potential gains in terms of emotional support and informational support offered to parents when networking online. This study has identified cyber lurking behaviours found within a major Australian parenting website, the Raising Children Network (RCN). It is hoped that these findings will assist moderators and website developers of the RCN and of other online networks to adopt new website features, user policies, and guidelines that will better encourage interactions and interconnections amongst members of the RCN forums.

Furthermore, it is vital that moderators of parenting websites are well informed of the importance and developmental benefits of ECE. With findings suggesting parental decision making is influenced by online interactions or the lack of them, the promotion and support for parental use of ECE within social networking forums is a crucial online responsibility of parenting website providers. This is quite significant for the RCN, considering that it is a parenting website supported and endorsed by the Australian government's Department of Social Services. Optimising social capital developed through this resource can also enhance parenting support. However, it cannot be assumed that users will engage in socially responsible behaviours without clear advice, guidelines and the close monitoring and support of forum moderators. Such monitoring will also enable moderators to provide replies to questions or posts when users have failed to attract a response to their post within a certain timeframe.

6.4 Summary of recommendations

Individuals can feel that their stressful circumstances are not validated when their calls for advice or support are read but do not receive a response. Thus, websites that facilitate platforms for user social networking may need to consider adopting policies guiding online social media interactions that support user commitment and compulsion to enact real helping behaviours (Scaffidi Abbate, Boca, Spadaro, & Romano, 2014). Furthermore, recommendations exist for forum moderators of parenting websites to monitor user posts and render assistance where a user has not received a timely peer response. Moderators may also require formal training in the social sciences and welfare, to ensure that they are not affected by bystander barriers that would render users vulnerable to neglect of their potentially perilous circumstances and inevitable failure to receive adequate advice or referral. Participants of online social support groups value prompt and convenient feedback and support (Evans, Donelle, & Hume-Loveland, 2012).

Technical forum facilities such as prompt email notifications informing forum users that they have received a reply to their post may assist in extending and consolidating support online and the potential expansion of the social capital attained through online networking (De Souza & Preece, 2004). Software facilities that give forum members an indication of the number of users currently active on the forum (De Souza & Preece, 2004) may further encourage forum activity. Specifically, De Souza and Preece (2004) state that "the ease with which community members interact with each other and with the technology will depend on how well designers support sociability and usability" (p. 587).

Digital bystanders can often refrain from involvement for fear of retribution (Wong-Lo & Bullock, 2014) or making a mistake (Hudson & Bruckman, 2004); and further research needs to be conducted to determine whether this phenomenon inhibits the interactions of members within online parenting communities. The design and availability of community resources have a direct impact on child and family outcomes (Bowes & Hayes, 2004). Therefore, social media sites that aim to serve families must ensure that users fulfil their responsibilities to their online peers. Policies guiding online etiquette, and cyber good Samaritan and upstander behaviours, need to be adopted and consistently reinforced by parenting social media websites. Furthermore, policies guiding comparison making will be useful to minimise depressive symptoms (Evans, Donelle, & Hume-Loveland, 2012) and or feelings of inadequacy for vulnerable parents online (Coyne et al., 2017).

Certain social networking behaviours by families, from cyber lurking and passive support, thus need to change if such forums are to offer parents the social support they are seeking and the social capital they have sought to gain through parenting websites and online networking forums. Christopherson (2007) applies the Social Identity model of Deindividualization Effects (SIDE), which can work to mediate individual anonymity, and better facilitate equality and a sense of belonging to a community, in order to strengthen supportive online group behaviours. Thus, innovations and uniformity in cyber community etiquette may assist in altering passive support behaviours (Drentea & Moren-Cross, 2005) and shifting the mindset of online social media participants regarding their online social responsibilities (Polder-Verkiel, 2012), which could improve intervention behaviours (Latané & Darley, 1970) online.

Innovation in online social networking challenges traditional assumptions that suggest that the internet provides users with effortless access to a multitude of social support and information at any time. Although the internet has enabled users to overcome previous

79

geographical barriers to gaining social networking and support, internet users such as those involved in raising children today are still standing at the foot of a digital mountain which they must climb over in order to effectively attain the social, informational and emotional support they are seeking online. Insights gained from the present study offer solutions on how to overcome these barriers by establishing more supportive approaches to the moderation of interactions between network members. Online social networkers are still in the embryonic stage of becoming effective and supportive members with their cyber communities. There remains a great deal of learning that needs to be facilitated by parenting websites, and that of their forum moderators, which would enlighten community members as to their online social responsibilities, and guide their interactions toward good cyber Samaritanism.

References

ABS. (2016). *8146.0 - Household Use of Information Technology, Australia, 2014-15.* Retrieved from http://www.abs.gov.au/ausstats/abs@.nsf/0/ACC2D18CC958BC7BCA2568A9001393 AE?Opendocument.

Ancheta Arrabal, A. (2015). Comparing early childhood education and care from a rightsbased approach. *Revista española de educación comparada*(25), 47-63. doi:10.5944/reec.25.2015.14783

Anker, A. E., & Feeley, T. H. (2011). Are nonparticipants in prosocial behavior merely innocent bystanders? *Health communication, 26*(1), 13-24. doi:http://dx.doi.org/10.1080/10410236.2011.527618

Bambina, A. (2007). *Online social support: the interplay of social networks and computer-mediated communication.* New York: Cambria press.

Bartholomew, M. K., Schoppe-Sullivan, S. J., Glassman, M., Kamp Dush, C. M., & Sullivan, J. M. (2012). New parents' Facebook use at the transition to parenthood. *Family relations, 61*(3), 455-469. doi:10.1111/j.1741-3729.2012.00708.x

Baxter, J., & Hand, K. (2013). *Access to early childhood education in Australia* (Research Report No. 24). Retrieved from Melbourne: http://observgo.uquebec.ca/observgo/fichiers/78979_Australie-access.pdf

Berry, D., Blair, C., Willoughby, M., Garrett-Peters, P., Vernon-Feagans, L., Mills-Koonce, W. R., & Investigators, F. L. P. K. (2016). Household chaos and children's cognitive and socio-emotional development in early childhood: Does childcare play a buffering role? *Early Childhood Research Quarterly, 34*, 115-127. doi:doi.org/10.1016/j.ecresq.2015.09.003

Biddle, N. (2007). Indigenous Australians and preschool education: Who is attending? *Australian Journal of Early Childhood, 32*(3), 9. Retrieved from http://search.informit.com.au.simsrad.net.ocs.mq.edu.au/documentSummary;dn=2007 10368;res=IELAPA> ISSN: 0312-5033

Bowes, J., & Grace, R. (Eds.). (2009). *Contexts and consequences: impacts on children, families and communities* (Vol. 3). Australia Oxford University Press.

Bowes, J., Grace, R., & Hayes, A. (2012). *Contexts and Consequences: Impacts on Children, Families and Communities*. Australia: Oxford.

Bowes, J., Watson, J., & Pearson, E. (2012). Families as a context for children. In J. Bowes, R. Grace, & K. Hodge (Eds.), *Children, families and communities: Contexts and consequences* (pp. 91-110). Australia: Oxford.

Britt Drugli, M., & Mari Undheim, A. (2012). Relationships between young children in full-time day care and their caregivers: a qualitative study of parental and caregiver perspectives. *Early Child Development & Care, 182*(9), 1155-1165. doi:10.1080/03004430.2011.602190

Bronfenbrenner, U. (2009). *The ecology of human development: Experiments by nature and design*. Cambridge: Harvard University Press.

Carlon, S., Stephenson, J., & Carter, M. (2015). Parent Perspectives on Sources of Information About Autism Spectrum Disorder Interventions in Australia. *Australasian Journal of Special Education, 39*(2), 113-127. doi:doi.org/10.1017/jse.2015.9

Christopherson, K. M. (2007). The positive and negative implications of anonymity in Internet social interactions:"On the Internet, Nobody Knows You're a Dog". *Computers in Human Behavior, 23*(6), 3038-3056. doi:org/10.1016/j.chb.2006.09.001

Coley, R. L., Lombardi, C. M., Sims, J., & Votruba-Drzal, E. (2013). Early education and care experiences and cognitive skills development: A comparitive perspective between Australian and American children. *Family Matters*(93), 36-49. Retrieved from

http://simsrad.net.ocs.mq.edu.au/login?url=http://search.ebscohost.com/login.aspx?dir
ect=true&db=aph&AN=93275209&site=ehost-live

Combs, J. P., & Onwuegbuzie, A. J. (2010). Describing and illustrating data analysis in mixed research. *International Journal of Education, 2*(2), 1. doi:10.5296/ije.v2i2.526

Coyne, S. M., McDaniel, B. T., & Stockdale, L. A. (2017). "Do you dare to compare?" Associations between maternal social comparisons on social networking sites and parenting, mental health, and romantic relationship outcomes. *Computers in Human Behavior, 70*, 335-340. doi:http://dx.doi.org/10.1016/j.chb.2016.12.081

Craig, L., & Powell, A. (2013). Non-parental childcare, time pressure and the gendered division of paid work, domestic work and parental childcare. *Community, Work & Family, 16*(1), 100-119. doi:10.1080/13668803.2012.722013

Czarniawska, B. (2014). *Social Science Research: From field to desk*. London: Sage.

Daneback, K., & Plantin, L. (2015). Research on parenthood and the Internet: Themes and trends. *Cyberpsychology: Journal of Psychosocial Research on Cyberspace, 2*(2). Retrieved from https://journals.muni.cz/cyberpsychology/article/view/4213/3255

Davis, K. E. (2015). *The information experience of new mothers in social media: A grounded theory study*. Queensland University of Technology, QLD. Retrieved from QUT ePrints http://eprints.qut.edu.au/86784/ (86784)

Denham, S. A., Bassett, H. H., & Zinsser, K. (2012). Early childhood teachers as socializers of young children's emotional competence. *Early Childhood Education Journal, 40*(3), 137-143. doi:10.1007/s10643-004-1424-6

Doty, J. L., & Dworkin, J. (2014). Online social support for parents: a critical review. *Marriage & Family Review, 50*(2), 174-198. doi:http://dx.doi.org/10.1080/01494929.2013.834027

Douglass, A., & Gittell, J. H. (2012). Transforming Professionalism: Relational Bureaucracy and Parent-Teacher Partnerships in Child Care Settings. *Journal of Early Childhood Research, 10*(3), 267-281. doi:10.1177/1476718X12442067

Drentea, P., & Moren-Cross, J. L. (2005). Social capital and social support on the web: the case of an internet mother site. *Sociology of health & illness, 27*(7), 920-943. doi:10.1111/j.1467-9566.2005.00464.x

Ess, C. (2002). Ethical decision-making and Internet research: Recommendations from the aoir ethics working committee. *Readings in virtual research ethics: Issues and controversies,* 27-44. Retrieved from http://www.fsa.ulaval.ca/cours/mrk-64662/popup/%C3%A9thique%20de%20la%20recherche%20dans%20SL/ethicsSL.pdf

Evans, M., Donelle, L., & Hume-Loveland, L. (2012). Social support and online postpartum depression discussion groups: A content analysis. *Patient education and counseling, 87*(3), 405-410. doi:https://doi.org/10.1016/j.pec.2011.09.011

Fenech, M. (2013). Quality early childhood education for my child or for all children? Parents as activists for equitable, high-quality early childhood education in Australia. *Australasian Journal of Early Childhood, 38*(4), 92-98. Retrieved from http://simsrad.net.ocs.mq.edu.au/login?url=http://search.ebscohost.com/login.aspx?direct=true&db=aph&AN=95060980&site=ehost-live

Fordham, L., Gibson, F., & Bowes, J. (2012). Information and professional support: key factors in the provision of family-centred early childhood intervention services. *Child: Care, Health & Development, 38*(5), 647-653. doi:10.1111/j.1365-2214.2011.01324.x

Government, A. (2016). Work, Training, Study test for Child Care Benefit. Retrieved from https://www.humanservices.gov.au/customer/enablers/work-training-study-test-child-care-benefit

Grace, R., Hayes, A., & Wise, S. (2017). *Child development in context.* South Melbourne, Victoria: Oxford University Press.

Hall, W., & Irvine, V. (2009). E-communication among mothers of infants and toddlers in a community-based cohort: A content analysis. *Journal of advanced nursing, 65*(1), 175-183. doi:10.1111/j.1365-2648.2008.04856.x

Hsieh, H.-F., & Shannon, S. E. (2005). Three approaches to qualitative content analysis. *Qualitative health research, 15*(9), 1277-1288. doi:10.1177/1049732305276687

Hudson, J. M., & Bruckman, A. S. (2009). The bystander effect: A lens for understanding patterns of participation. *The Journal of the Learning Sciences, 13*(2), 165-195. doi:http://dx.doi.org/10.1207/s15327809jls1302_2

Ionescu, M. (2015). Organization Spotlight: The Power of an Association in Early Childhood Education and Care: ISSA--An Engine for Advocacy, Capacity Building, and Creating a Growing Learning Community. *Childhood Education, 91*(5), 390-394. doi:10.1080/00094056.2015.1090856

Irvine, S., Davidson, C., Veresov, N., Adams, M., & Devi, A. (2015). Lenses and Lessons: Using three different research perspectives in early childhood education research. *Призмы концепций: опыт анализа исследования в области дошкольного образования с точки зрения трех различных подходов, 11*(3), 75-85. doi:10.17759/chp.2015110307

Jackiewicz, S., Saggers, S., & Frances, K. (2011). Equity of access: Requirements of Indigenous families and communities to ensure equitable access to government-approved childcare settings in Australia. *Australasian Journal of Early Childhood, 36*(3), 100. Retrieved from https://search.informit.com.au/documentSummary;dn=342599737948410;res

Johnson, R., & Christensen, L. (2014). *Educational research: Quantitative and qualitative approaches* (5 ed.). Thousand Oaks, California: SAGE Publications.

Krieg, S., Smith, K. A., & Davis, K. (2014). Exploring the dance of early childhood educational leadership. *Australasian Journal of Early Childhood, 39(1)*(1), 73-80. Retrieved from http://search.informit.com.au/documentSummary;dn=192637473473137;res=IELAPA

Krippendorff, K. (2012). *Content analysis: An introduction to its methodology*: Sage.

Lansford, J. E., Ceballo, R., Abbey, A., & Stewart, A. J. (2001). Does family structure matter? A comparison of adoptive, two-parent biological, single-mother, stepfather, and stepmother households. *Journal of Marriage and family, 63*(3), 840-851. doi:10.1111/j.1741-3737.2001.00840.x

Latané, B., & Darley, J. M. (1970). *The unresponsive bystander: Why doesn't he help?* USA: Meredith.

Latané, B., & Nida, S. (1981). Ten years of research on group size and helping. *Psychological Bulletin, 89*(2), 308. doi:http://dx.doi.org/10.1037/0033-2909.89.2.308

Madge, C., & O'Connor, H. (2006). Parenting gone wired: empowerment of new mothers on the internet? *Social & Cultural Geography, 7*(02), 199-220. doi:http://dx.doi.org/10.1080/14649360600600528

Maguire, B., & Hayes, A. (2012). Access to preschool education in the year before full-time school. *Annual statistical report 2011,* 57. Retrieved from https://www.researchgate.net/profile/John_Ainley/publication/254581559_Children's_numeracy_skills/links/53e9b6f60cf2dc24b3cac321/Childrens-numeracy-skills.pdf#page=71

Marshall, N. L., Robeson, W. W., Tracy, A. J., Frye, A., & Roberts, J. (2013). Subsidized child care, maternal employment and access to quality, affordable child care. *Early Childhood Research Quarterly, 28*(4), 808-819. doi:http://dx.doi.org/10.1016/j.ecresq.2013.07.008

McDaniel, B. T., Coyne, S. M., & Holmes, E. K. (2012). New mothers and media use: Associations between blogging, social networking, and maternal well-being. *Maternal and child health journal, 16*(7), 1509-1517. doi:10.1007/s10995-011-0918-2

Mukherji, P., & Albon, D. (2014). *Research methods in Early Childhood. An introductory guide*. London: Sage.

Nichols, S. (2014). Mothers and fathers resourcing early learning and development. *Australasian Journal of Early Childhood, 39*(4), 64-71. Retrieved from http://simsrad.net.ocs.mq.edu.au/login?url=http://search.ebscohost.com/login.aspx?direct=true&db=aph&AN=100402438&site=ehost-live

Nieuwboer, C. C., Fukkink, R. G., & Hermanns, J. M. (2013). Peer and professional parenting support on the Internet: a systematic review. *Cyberpsychology, Behavior, and Social Networking, 16*(7), 518-528. doi:10.1089/cyber.2012.0547

O'Connor, M., Gray, S., Tarasuik, J., O'Connor, E., Kvalsvig, A., Incledon, E., & Goldfeld, S. (2016). Preschool attendance trends in Australia: Evidence from two sequential population cohorts. *Early Childhood Research Quarterly*. doi:https://doi.org/10.1016/j.ecresq.2015.11.004

Paterson, B. L., Brewer, J., & Stamler, L. L. (2013). Engagement of parents in on-line social support interventions. *Journal of pediatric nursing, 28*(2), 114-124. doi:http://dx.doi.org/10.1016/j.pedn.2012.05.001

Pedersen, S., & Smithson, J. (2010). Membership and activity in an online parenting community. *Handbook of research on discourse behavior and digital communication: Language structures and social interaction*, 88-103. Retrieved from http://openair.rgu.ac.uk

Plantin, L., & Daneback, K. (2009). Parenthood, information and support on the internet. A literature review of research on parents and professionals online. *BMC Family Practice, 10*(1), 34. doi:https://doi.org/10.1186/1471-2296-10-34

Rouleau, L., de Rond, M., & Musca, G. (2014). From the ethnographic turn to new forms of organizational ethnography. *Journal of Organizational Ethnography, 3*(1), 2-9. doi:10.1108/JOE-02-2014-0006

Sarkadi, A., & Bremberg, S. (2005). Socially unbiased parenting support on the Internet: a cross-sectional study of users of a large Swedish parenting website. *Child: care, health and development, 31*(1), 43-52. doi:10.1111/j.1365-2214.2005.00475.x

Scaffidi Abbate, C., Boca, S., Spadaro, G., & Romano, A. (2014). Priming effects on commitment to help and on real helping behavior. *Basic and Applied Social Psychology, 36*(4), 347-355. doi:http://dx.doi.org/10.1080/01973533.2014.922089

September, S. J., Rich, E. G., & Roman, N. V. (2016). The role of parenting styles and socio-economic status in parents' knowledge of child development. *Early Child Development and Care, 186*(7), 1060-1078. doi:http://dx.doi.org.simsrad.net.ocs.mq.edu.au/10.1080/03004430.2015.1076399

UN. (1989). Convention on the Rights of the Child: Entered into force Sep. 2 1990. Retrieved from http://www.ohchr.org/EN/ProfessionalInterest/Pages/CRC.aspx.

Veisson, M. (2015). Professionalism of Preschool Teachers: A Cross-Cultural Study [PowerPoint Presentation].

Appendix A

Topic 1: Schooling and education

This topic was established to reflect user discussion regarding schooling and education from birth to secondary education.

Poster Code name	Post title	Post Views	Post replies
RC0111	Nursery rhymes and songs for toddlers	1000	3
RC0117	daycare	821	2
RC0118	fear of going to childcare	1400	3
RC0137	Where can I find study tips to help my kids?	557	1
RC0140	children activities	2100	7
RC0152	SA High Schools Small Special Classes	239	0
RC0165	Schools in Brisbane	575	0
RC0179	Trophies	779	1
RC0183	Advice about high schools near Port Douglas please	678	1
RC0308	Maths tutor - primary school	1000	2
RC0313	Supportive and inclusive secondary schools in Melbourne	466	0
RC0316	Supportive High School	512	1
RC0324	School gifted and talented program?	1000	1
RC0346	Schools suspending children	2900	3
RC0361	MAYBE MOVING TO BATHURST. ...school recommendations	539	0
RC0376	Suitable State High Schools in Perth	486	0
RC0386	Children school assignments	650	1
RC0105	When to start school	450	1

Topic 2: Autism/ABA

This table is a collation of posts by users concerned that their child or sibling may be autistic, parents whose children were recently diagnosed with autism, or families requesting information about autism, particularly information about applied behaviour analysis (ABA).

Poster name	Code	Post title	Post Views	Post replies
RC0016		Query regarding ABA	341	1
RC0018		17mo displaying red flags for ASD what to do?	1100	5
RC0037		Frustrated with trying to correct behavior while being sensitive to ASD needs	774	1
RC0064		Just found out my 11yo has ***	685	2
RC0084		Younger brother suffering parents NOT supporting or helping	1,500	4
RC0107		Home Help/Cleaning for Carer Parents of ASD????	1600	4
RC0053		Our baby boy turned out to be autistic and we are shattered	1000	1
RC0114		Sleep issues with my 4 year old autistic Boy	304	0
RC0121		Music Therapy	1700	1
RC0130		Should I Get My Son Reassessed?	654	2
RC0152		ASD son's Father Having Baby With Current Wife	1500	6
RC0174		Newly diagnosed 2 yo boy	2600	5
RC0018		Mum of 17mo boy displaying red flags for autism	616	1
RC0181		How to become an autism carer	452	0
RC0190		Moving to Melbourne from Adelaide	382	0
RC0222		Advice on Potty training a 6 year old Autistic boy	901	3
RC0302		ABA therapy cost...and more questions about ABA	1400	4
RC0319		Anxiety	1300	2
RC0343		PR with Autistic Son	476	0
RC0350		Problem about confronted by these parents	2400	2
RC0352		Is my Child Austistic? Please Help	956	2
RC0023		Second baby after ASD diagnosis	798	1
RC0358		HELP! ASD Only Child (teen) expecting new sibling - NOT COPING	614	0
RC0374		4yo Son just diagnosed - Looking for Advice on ABA centers in/around...	729	0
RC0379		2.5year old diagnosed with ASD yesterday	1600	5

RC0382	4yo girl diagnosed last year, just found this forum	676	0
RC0193	Aggressive Behavior	942	0
RC0194	Distance Ed for child with ASD	513	0
RC0199	4yo girl just diagnosed... Looking for some hope!	2200	4
RC0201	Advice on younger sibling copying asd behavior	419	0
RC0202	Swimming and my Asd 6 yrs	429	0
RC0203	Hi, needing help with regard to respite care	1900	1

Topic 3: Challenging Issues

User posts about challenging issues such as children's behaviour and difficulties with routine times were assigned to the challenging issues category. Challenging issues were categorised where the user indicated that the behaviour was interfering with their own well-being and or overall quality of family life. Posts which presented personal conflicts, and conflicts within interpersonal relationships were also placed in this category.

Original Poster Codename	Post title	Number of Views	Number of replies
RC0002	Teen speeding tickets, fines, tow bills	376	2
RC0081	Overwhelemed by demanding behaviour	743	1
RC0103	Desperate need of sleep! Help!	447	1
RC0108	How to get rid of games for my 14-year-old son?	2900	13
RC0113	Full time stepmum of 2, no kids of own, behavioural problems	271	0
RC0119	Bedwetting - 8yr & nearly 10yr old	12000	15
RC0133	Teenagers having sex	1400	3
RC0139	What have children done before they go to bed?	1700	7
RC0153	Bedwetting...7 year old now ok	646	0
RC0155	My 9yr daughter keeps running away	1300	0
RC0169	5 year old that's a terrible sleeper - help!!!	874	1
RC0178	11 year old daughter odd behaviour of just rude??	1500	0
RC0184	13 y/o daughter want to spend all her time at her friends house	822	0
RC0187	14y/o daughter self harming and making poor friend choices	731	1

RC0195	9 Yrs Old Boy Misbehavior And Unattentive	1100	0
RC2197	Rude disrespectful 12yr old - being rude at school	1900	5
RC0205	13-year-old girl wants to go to city to meet friends	802	1
RC0208	Help Is It Normal Behaviour??	602	1
RC0215	Drop offs - at our wit's end :(	638	1
RC0218	My 5 year old bedtime/sleep routine is CRAZY!!!! And its driving me…	763	1
RC0224	verbal abusive 15 year old	769	1
RC0226	My 14yr old daughter and my partner of 7 years always arguing and…	579	1
RC0228	What steps to take a 5-year-old is being defiant?	1200	3
RC0312	3 year old son been a terror	1900	3
RC0323	Swaddle help!	966	0
RC0329	disrespect to teachers	1900	2
RC0332	Going out of my mind.	1300	3
RC0333	Cranky, Moody, Defiant, Middle child.	550	0
RC0335	At my wit's end!	1000	1
RC0336	6YO whinging and whining	1700	6
RC0337	Tantrums	423	0
RC0339	My 4 year old will not poo on the toilet/potty!	1300	3
RC0229	Lets talk about our Only Children	8400	27
RC0348	10 year old with two wetting accidents	3000	1
RC0024	Behaviour Change Clinic or Boot Camps	1100	1
RC0355	12 year old girl home alone overnight?	1600	7
RC0357	12 yr old girl needing birth control???	2400	6
RC0359	Where do I get help	958	2
RC0360	Mr 14 years is wagging and lying to us	2000	5
RC0362	13 y/o wants body piercing	4600	9
RC0368	HELP!! need advice to help get my profoundly deaf son to settle…	538	0
RC0383	4 year old suddenly scared to sleep alone after holiday	1100	1
RC0384	Tearing my hair out with teenagers	570	0
RC0385	4 years old sleeping issue	1200	3
RC0351	Teenage Bedtimes	1900	7
RC0207	Son No Allowed To Play Footy with his Mates	1700	1

RC0311	Too much parenting	1200	2
RC0342	Discussing pornography with teen boys	1300	1
RC0349	in trouble from the neighbour	3100	7
RC0356	Miserable 13 year old boy	2100	4
RC0363	Teenage daughter lonely n low self esteem	739	1
RC2256	Didn't know what my kids were into until...	760	1

Topic 4: Fertility, pregnancy and infants

This category represents discussions regarding conception, prenatal concerns and, postnatal

issues.

Topic Code	Poster Code name	Post title	Post Views	Post replies
Topic 4	RC0005	Pregnancy sleeping position, help!	1700	2
Topic 4	RC0006	feeling sleepy in pregnancy? Is it normal in Pregnancy?	393	1
Topic 4	RC0027	Difficult 10 month eater	1500	5
Topic 4	RC0032	How to buy new born baby suit	7800	6
Topic 4	RC0073	Worries about fertility	1,100	2
Topic 4	RC0083	Baby names.. Idea's??	8100	27
Topic 4	RC0088	Child monitoring	319	2
Topic 4	RC0088	Pregnancy and swimming	337	2
Topic 4	RC0096	Need help with breast pump	234	0
Topic 4	RC0101	Mmr injection 4 days prior to conception	209	0
Topic 4	RC0115	Baby	663	1
Topic 4	RC0126	Surrogacy, looking for answers!	292	1
Topic 4	RC0128	IVF rollercoaster	8400	16
Topic 4	RC0129	Reduced Immunity for baby	182	0
Topic 4	RC0131	what baby bottles are best	4900	10
Topic 4	RC0141	Wanting another baby…	1700	4
Topic 4	RC0156	Twin Prams	4500	6
Topic 4	RC0172	what about expectant Mums?	1700	3
Topic 4	RC0185	Travel insurance while pregnant	1400	1
Topic 4	RC0189	Post Birth recurring issue	563	0
Topic 4	RC0141	Expressing Breast Milk	3000	15
Topic 4	RC0213	How is you baby sleeping in the heat of summer	2400	5
Topic 4	RC0304	which Avent nipple size I have to use to my daughter?	1300	1
Topic 4	RC0306	Pregnant 4 months after csection	722	2
Topic 4	RC0338	Introduction / should I be worried?	1200	5

Topic 5: Child Development and Health

Topic 5 encompasses posts that reflect parental concerns for their children's health and development (other than Autism/ABA).

Topic Code	Poster Code name	Post title	Post Views	Post replies
Topic 5	RC0029	Paediatrician visits	1200	2
Topic 5	RC0056	Does my daughter really need eyeglasses?	1700	4
Topic 5	RC0089	Fear of dentists!	1000	9
Topic 5	RC0091	4 year old son acts differently at school then at home	1100	3
Topic 5	RC0099	Weighted blankets?	1500	6
Topic 5	RC0106	How to teach a 5 year old basic math	560	1
Topic 5	RC0124	Could mould have caused a rash?	1000	1
Topic 5	RC0135	Parents helping kids with homework	3400	6
Topic 5	RC0138	Child having trouble in preschool but not at home	383	1
Topic 5	RC0147	6 YO Boy social skills need help	2200	6
Topic 5	RC0158	I need as much advise as I can get!	535	0
Topic 5	RC0163	How do I know if a kid is Obese or not?	634	1
Topic 5	RC0163	How to avoid junk food	471	1
Topic 5	RC0196	Is Biomedical Treatment in Sydney covered under facsia funding?	751	2
Topic 5	RC0206	Muscle gain for boys	747	2
Topic 5	RC0211	Recent diagnosis adhd	656	0
Topic 5	RC0301	Tummy Pain	370	0
Topic 5	RC0301	Ongoing tummy pain....	331	0
Topic 5	RC0315	My 4 year old boy wants to be a girl	1700	5
Topic 5	RC0317	10yo daughter becoming bit of a loner	4500	5
Topic 5	RC0327	Am i being too pushy??	1500	1
Topic 5	RC0328	9 year old daughter with unhealthy obsession	2500	3
Topic 5	RC0347	Hair washing	1700	3
Topic 5	RC0163	Childhood obseity	467	3
Topic 5	RC0377	Not just impacted bowel...now for a bone scan :(	6500	58
Topic 5	RC0102	Adolescent Mental Health	318	0
Topic 5	RC0318	First Period	2700	5
Topic 5	RC0116	Toddler Behaviour	746	2
Topic 5	RC0314	Upside Down & Backwards	1100	3

Topic 6: Family Matters

The Family Matters category represents posts regarding issues with family structure, parent relationships or foster parents. The category also reflects messages uploaded by grandparents.

Topic Code	Original Poster Code name	Post title	Post Views	Post replies
Topic 6	RC0014	Childless 26yr old struggling to live 2days/week with partner and 6yr old son	1000	5
Topic 6	RC0031	Raising Children	3100	7
Topic 6	RC0046	Separated But still living under one roof	69000	23
Topic 6	RC0097	Teaching gentle play	720	2
Topic 6	RC0123	New here, but long time mum with a question!	521	0
Topic 6	RC0443	Seeking Step Mum Support Group in Brisbane	4100	25
Topic 6	RC0161	Being a stepmum	643	1
Topic 6	RC0166	Struggling batty step mum	296	0
Topic 6	RC0167	Father of our child diagnosed with depression...I have no one to talk…	356	0
Topic 6	RC0168	Help am I over reacting	581	0
Topic 6	RC0191	Custody, protection	842	1
Topic 6	RC0209	Advice for new access arrangements/supporting partner	1200	1
Topic 6	RC0217	Shared care and other ex partners	573	0
Topic 6	RC0217	Blended families with multiple fathers	593	0
Topic 6	RC0220	Separated under one roof - parenting examples	671	1
Topic 6	RC0321	Resenting Partner	1200	3
Topic 6	RC0325	So I left... Now he gets shared custody?	544	0
Topic 6	RC0326	Foster Care - Agency Frustration	802	0
Topic 6	RC0330	Grandma raising grandchild social network	9500	11
Topic 6	RC0334	Happy Valentines Day Grandchildren	491	0
Topic 6	RC0340	Worried about the threat of abuse.	984	3
Topic 6	RC0345	Is my husband neglecting my 7 year old?	1400	2
Topic 6	RC0371	recently separated advice	931	1
Topic 6	RC0381	Building Relationships with the "New Partner"	484	0
Topic 6	RC1229	Grandparent carer of child who has a mother with mental illness	961	2
Topic 6	RC1192	Parenting an only child (20 month old)	395	0

Topic 7: Other interests

All posts that reflected topics of interest such as travel, shopping or babysitting were placed in

category seven.

Topic Code	Original Poster Code name	Post title	Post Views	Post replies
Topic 7	RC0011	North Brisbane's Mother's group	411	3
Topic 7	RC0023	How many active members on this forum?	991	3
Topic 7	RC0072	Facebook Dads Community	1,200	1
Topic 7	RC0125	Hi, I did not see an "Introduce Yourself" section...	245	0
Topic 7	RC0130	What is the point	527	0
Topic 7	RC0144	Best parental control software?	561	0
Topic 7	RC0145	Always listen to music baby Finger Family from the iPad?	224	0
Topic 7	RC0148	Why My Boy Likes a Tank Shape Plush Toy?	382	0
Topic 7	RC0149	Electronics Use	370	1
Topic 7	RC0151	looking for a suport group we can attend in perth wa for help how to deal with this situastion...	460	0
Topic 7	RC0160	Mean school mums	1100	2
Topic 7	RC0164	Frustrated Mum	487	0
Topic 7	RC0176	Looking for parents with kids in western Sydney	1600	2
Topic 7	RC0163	Hi everyone...	810	1
Topic 7	RC0214	Would you rather sell or give away your kids near new clothes?	742	1
Topic 7	RC0214	How much do you spend on your childrens clothes?	544	1
Topic 7	RC0344	Coming back to Melbourne from Sweden	395	0
Topic 7	RC0364	When Is My Child Ready for a Smartphone?	1300	4
Topic 7	RC0365	Stressed	452	0
Topic 7	RC0367	Education Child Games Mobile Options; Android/iOS VS Quality	777	0
Topic 7	RC0370	Need travel advice and tips!	394	0
Topic 7	RC0375	Babysiter Supply	379	0
Topic 7	RC0375	A Question About Demand for Babysitters	245	0
Topic 7	RC0369	Trophies for ceremony!	592	0
Topic 7	RC0320	Cute Idea	1600	1
Topic 7	RC0154	Feeling lost	335	0
Topic 7	RC0186	Sleepovers	554	0
Topic 7	RC0310	Friends not playing nicely	3400	4

Appendix B

Correspondence between RC0187 and RC0188

Date: March 22, 2016

Post title: 14y/o daughter self harming and making poor friend choices

Posting: My daughter has gone from loving school to hating it, she has made friends with a group of girls that hate school, constantly get suspended, a couple of the girls even have police records, my daughter has been taken in by this group, being the type of child that has always struggled to make friends she has loved having lots of friends.

But today she has been suspended for the second time, her friends think it fantastic and that its all a joke.

I don't want to tell her to stop being around these friends, I just remind her to make choices that are true to what she wants, and make safe choices, it's getting me no where, today when I collected her from school after being suspended I noticed cuts up her arm, she said that she did it because she thought we would move her schools and she wouldn't see her best friends again, she also had told me she has done it about 12 months ago, before she had these friends and was struggling to make friends. I have made an appointment for her to see the student guidance counsellor tomorrow but she is adamant she will not go. I'm heart broken I cannot reach out to my child. Any advice on any of the above would be very welcomed please.

Respondent: RC0188

Date: April 3, 2016

Posting: Wow [RC0187] you have so much going on, I can imagine how distressing this is. When one of my kids was needing help but refusing it I gave them a couple of options to choose between, like seeing a counsellor at school, our family doctor or a private counsellor. I'm not sure if that could work. The need to belong is so powerful at this age, so I think you're right not to try and pull her away from these friends because that will make her only cling harder and push further away from you. If only our kids didn't feel the need to learn about life the hard way! My only other suggestion is to keep reminding her of her dreams and explain that you're there to support her to reach them. That can sometimes help kids realise they're in with a bad bunch without you having to tell them that."

Appendix C

Post by RC0155

Hi I am at my wits end my husband walked out on me and 3 children this was a relief on one hand as he is an abusive alcoholic. The problem is my 9 yr old daughter has started running away but not to her dads as You would imagine in fact she has done the same whilst she has been staying with him. At first I thought it was because she was rebelling didn't want to do any thing that was asked of her but it even happens when we have had a good day no demands no cross words. She is extremely bright and is doing well at school although she doesnt have any real friends. She has started humming quietly to her self all the time as if she is trying to block out her surrounding. I will pick all three up from school/kindy she's happy had a good day I will stop at a junction and she jumps out. I will be getting the younger two ready for bed or making dinner hear the door and she's off. Some nights I have spent up to 3 hrs driving around the streets with the 2 children asleep in the car looking for her. Early morning driving around with children not fed and still in pyjamas way past school start time Trying desperately to find her. I've found her under a neighbours car, hiding in doorways. I dread going to sleep in case she Goes and I don't know. I am so afraid something will happen to her When I do find her she goes into a rage and I struggle to get her into the car one time I had locked the car doors she kicked the windscreen so hard she cracked it. We live in a regional area no Counciling service to hand we have to wait for one to visit the town and the waiting list for an appointment is long. I know all the trauma and stress of her father leaving may be the trigger and certainly it's been hard but I just can't understand why she has reacted in such a dangerous way to run. How can I help her what should I say or do. if anyone has experience the same or similar behaviour I would love to know how you coped and where you got help

Appendix D

Survey respondent reasoning for not replying to posts online:

- I personally don't like to share too much

- Too many people have different views so i just keep mine to myself

- Just like reading them

- Not felt it necessary

- I keep my opinions to myself

- Too much effort

- Didn't feel appropriate

- I don't like that my reply can be seen by anyone. If it was private I might reply

- Don't know guess because I didn't know them that well

- Just haven't had anything to say

- Did not feel the need

- Don't like to post comments on social media

- Not sure

- It is more valuable to have "quality" friends rather than quantity. Safety issues and concerns in regard to connecting with people if you meet them online

- Too little time

- No real reason

- Just like to observe

- Waste of time

- Not interested in anonymous relationships. Prefer to talk face to face

- I avoid engaging in comments - too controversial

- I just believe that we do what we think is right and we connect with real people when we are worried or frustrated

- Not interested in doing so

- Other people are quick to give their input

- Didn't see the point really

- I don't like creating usernames & passwords for so many different sites

- Never felt inclined to

- Not interested

Appendix E

Online Survey

Stage 2 – Online survey questionnaire for parents

Project name: ***Early Childhood Matters: An exploration of family social media networking experiences*** (Ethics Approval No. 5201600370)

A) Thank you so much for taking the time to complete this survey.

Before starting the survey, please read the Participant Information Letter by clicking on this link:

[Participant information letter]

B) Please select the response that best describes your current circumstances.

Are you currently raising a child(ren)?

☐ YES

☐ NO

C) Are you an Australian citizen or do you have permanent residency status in Australia?

☐ YES

☐ NO

D) Are you currently 18 years old or over this age?

☐ YES

☐ NO

E) You have satisfied the pre-requisites for completing this survey.

Before proceeding, please confirm the following:

☐ I agree to participate in this survey

1) What state/territory do you currently live?

☐ NSW

☐ VIC

☐ SA

☐ WA

☐ TAS

☐ QLD

☐ NT

☐ ACT

2) Which of the following best describes where you currently live:

☐ City – metropolitan

☐ Regional town

☐ Rural community

☐ Isolated rural community

3) Please select the title that best describe you:

I am a:

☐   Mother

☐   Father

4) How many children are you currently raising?

☐   One child

☐   Two children

☐   Three children

☐   Four children

☐   Five or more children

5) How old are your children at present? Please select all applicable items based on the child/ren's current age(s):

☐   Child's age birth to 12 months

☐   Child's age 1- 2 years

☐   Child's age 3 – 4 years

☐   Child's age 5 years

☐   Children over 5 years. How many children do you have over the age of 5 years? Please specify below:

6) Which age range best represents your current age:

☐   Less than 20 years

☐   21-30 years

☐   31-40 years

☐   41- 50 years

☐   More than 51 years

7) Are you currently in paid employment?

☐ YES

☐ NO

8) [If yes] how many hours/days are you in paid employment:

   ☐ Less than 20 hours a week

   ☐ 20 hours a week

   ☐ Employed full-time five days a week

   ☐ Employed on a casual or irregular basis

9) Have your child/ren you are raising ever been cared for by a person other than yourself?

   ☐ YES

   ☐ NO

10) [If yes] Please indicate type of care used (select as many as applicable)

   ☐ Child's grandparent

   ☐ Child's other relative

   ☐ Family friend

   ☐ Family day carer

   ☐ Nanny

   ☐ Child care centre

   ☐ Preschool/Kindergarten

   ☐ Other – please provide details

_____

_____

11) How often did you use these childcare arrangements?

☐ Full time – Monday to Friday each week

☐ Part-time – Two to four days of the week

☐ One day a week regularly

☐ On a casual basis when there was a specific need during the week (e.g. appointment; illness; unplanned or unexpected emergency)

☐ Other please provide details

_____

12) Please finish this sentence:

Early   Childhood   Education   (ECE)   is   important   because…

_____

_____

_____

13) Do you believe every child should attend an early childhood centre such as a childcare centre or a preschool, before starting school?

☐ YES

☐ NO

Please tell us your reasons:

14) Please tell us your reasons

_____

15) To what extent do you agree with the following statements?

	Strongly agree	agree	Neither agree nor disagree	disagree	Strongly disagree
I believe that Early Childhood centres provide an ideal learning environment for children's development.	○	○	○	○	○
I have found my child's development improved by staying at home with me.	○	○	○	○	○
I have found my child's development improved by attending an Early Childhood centre.	○	○	○	○	○

The following questions focus on online social networking

16) How have you benefited from using social media? Choose as many as applicable.

☐ Provided me with new information

☐ Made me feel better knowing that I'm not alone as a parent

☐ Linked me with education services for my children

☐ Linked me with health services for my children .

☐ Assisted me in making decisions about my children's learning

☐ Helped me to network with other parents

☐ Gave me access to good advice from other parents in similar circumstances

☐ Other – Please explain briefly

_____

_____

17) To what extent do you agree with the following statement?

I found the online advice I received from other parents was more useful than the advice I received from health professionals:

- ☐ Strongly agree
- ☐ Somewhat agree
- ☐ Somewhat disagree
- ☐ Strongly disagree

18) Have you ever posted a note on social media?

- ☐ YES
- ☐ NO

19) [If 'yes'] What topic (s) did you focus on?

_____

_____

20) [If yes to Q17] Have you ever received a response to a post?

- ☐ YES
- ☐ NO

21) [If no to Q19] Have did you feel about not receiving a reply to your post?

_____

22) [If yes to Q19] Please describe how this information has helped you.

_____

_____

_____

23) In percentage terms, to what extent did you find social networking helpful in connecting with other parents?

24) In percentage terms, how confident are you about the reliability of social media to obtain information about parenting matters?

25) Have your child's or family's experiences been influenced by information you've gained through online social networking?

☐ Not at all

☐ A little

☐ Moderately

☐ Totally

26) Can you please tell us a little more about this?

27) If you have been reading posts regarding raising children, what topics have you looked at?

Choose all that apply:

- ☐ School and Education
- ☐ Children's Health including Autism
- ☐ Relationship with spouse
- ☐ Challenging children
- ☐ Fertility, Pregnancy & Infants
- ☐ Child development
- ☐ Relationships with immediate family members
- ☐ Relationships with extended family members

28) Other: Please specify:

_____

29) To what extent do you agree with the following?

	Not applicable	Agree	Disagree
Authoring a parenting blog has enabled me to meaningfully connect with other parents.	○	○	○
Reading parenting blogs has enabled me to relate to other parents.	○	○	○
Publishing status updates about my parenting experiences on social media has enabled me to meaningfully connect with other parents.	○	○	○
Reading status updates about the parenting experiences of other parents published on social media has enabled me to relate to other parents.	○	○	○

30) To what extent do you find online social media effective in terms of gaining information in regard to raising children?

Not at all effective   very effective

0   10   20   30   40   50   60   70   80   90   100

31) Have you ever replied to someone's blog or post online?

☐   Yes

☐   No

32) [If No to 28] Why not?

_____

33) [If   yes   to   28]   Please   provide   details

_____

34) How have you tried to establish contact with parents who you have networked with on the internet offline? (Select all that apply)

☐   No, I haven't tried to establish offline contact with any peer I've met online

☐   Meeting in person

☐   Text message

☐   Other social media

☐   Personal Email

☐   Phone call

35) Have you ever recommended online social media networking to other parents?

☐ Yes

☐ No

36) Select the response that you consider best matches your views about social media

	Strongly Disagree	Disagree	Somewhat disagree	Neither agree nor disagree	Somewhat agree	Agree	Strongly agree
Participation in social media has changed my views about parenting	○	○	○	○	○	○	○
Participation in social media has changed my views about using early childhood centres for my children.	○	○	○	○	○	○	○

37) Would you recommend online social media networking to other parents?

☐ Yes

☐ No

38) Please provide further information

_____

39) "THANK YOU", for taking the time to complete this survey!

Be in the running for two gold class movie tickets!

Enter your email address below.

Winners will be contacted via email

_____

Appendix F

Participant Information Sheet

Dear parents,

You are invited to participate in a study of **"An exploration of family social media networking experiences"** (Project Ref No: 5201600370). The aim of this study is to investigate family experiences of social media networking. Social networks play a big part in supporting families about early childhood education and care matters. Today's parents, in addition to local community health centres, family and friends, use social media to gain further insights, advice and suggestions regarding issues about raising their children. We are seeking your assistance in ascertaining the nature of your experiences through this survey.

How can you help?
Specifically, we are interested in the experiences of parents who are Australian citizens or permanent Australian residents currently living in Australia, and have children under the age of 6 years, to complete an online survey. The survey will take approximately 20 minutes to complete. The questions refer to social media networking in regard to gaining information about early childhood matters. It will ask for general information about yourself and your family to help us with analysing trends in the community.
Participation in the study is completely voluntary. You are free to choose whether or not to participate in this research and also withdraw from the study at any time without an explanation.

All data collected during this study will be stored securely at all times. Only Professor Manjula Waniganayake and I will have access to this data. The data collected and analysed will be presented in a thesis, and also used in any presentations and publications based on this research. This data will be presented in a way that no participant can be identified. By participating in this study, you can request a summary of the results of this research to be emailed to you.

Your participation is important to us. The knowledge gained through this research may assist early childhood educators to develop better relationships when working with families raising children.

The research is being conducted to meet the requirements for the degree of Master of Research under the supervision of Professor Manjula Waniganayake, at the Department of Educational Studies, at Macquarie University (email: manjula.waniganayake@mq.edu.au). If you would like any further information about this study, please do not hesitate to contact me by email at the address supplied in this statement.
Click here to start the survey

I would be very grateful if you could please pass on this invitation to other parents with young children such as yourself. The survey will close after Easter 2017.

With our sincere thanks for your participation in this research.

Suzana Stipanovic
Higher Degree Research candidate and Co-Investigator
suzana.stipanovic@hdr.mq.edu.au
Early Childhood, Department of Educational Studies, Faculty of Human Sciences

Appendix G

Ethics Approval

MACQUARIE
University

SUZANA NIKOLIC <suzana.nikolic@students.mq.edu.au>

RE: HS Ethics Application - Approved (5201600370)(Con/Met)
1 message

Fhs Ethics <fhs.ethics@mq.edu.au>   Tue, Jul 12, 2016 at 2:39 PM
To: Professor Manjula Waniganayake <manjula.waniganayake@mq.edu.au>
Cc: Mrs Suzana Stipanovic <suzana.nikolic@students.mq.edu.au>

Dear Professor Waniganayake,

Re: "Early Childhood Matters: Harnessing parents' perspectives through social media" (5201600370)

Thank you very much for your response. Your response has addressed the issues raised by the Faculty of Human Sciences Human Research Ethics Sub-Committee and approval has been granted, effective 12th July 2016. This email constitutes ethical approval only.

This research meets the requirements of the National Statement on Ethical Conduct in Human Research (2007). The National Statement is available at the following web site:

http://www.nhmrc.gov.au/_files_nhmrc/publications/attachments/e72.pdf.

The following personnel is authorised to conduct this research:

Mrs Suzana Stipanovic
Professor Manjula Waniganayake

Please note the following standard requirements of approval:

1.   The approval of this project is conditional upon your continuing compliance with the National Statement on Ethical Conduct in Human Research (2007).

2.   Approval will be for a period of five (5) years subject to the provision of annual reports.

Progress Report 1 Due: 12th July 2017
Progress Report 2 Due: 12th July 2018
Progress Report 3 Due: 12th July 2019
Progress Report 4 Due: 12th July 2020
Final Report Due: 12th July 2021

NB. If you complete the work earlier than you had planned you must submit a Final Report as soon as the work is completed. If the project has been discontinued or not commenced for any reason, you are also required to submit a Final Report for the project.

Progress reports and Final Reports are available at the following website:

http://www.research.mq.edu.au/current_research_staff/human_research_ethics/a
pplication_resources

3.   If the project has run for more than five (5) years you cannot renew approval for the project. You will need to complete and submit a Final Report and submit a new application for the project. (The five year limit on renewal of approvals allows the Sub-Committee to fully re-review research in an environment where legislation, guidelines and requirements

are continually changing, for example, new child protection and privacy laws).

4.   All amendments to the project must be reviewed and approved by the Sub-Committee before implementation. Please complete and submit a Request for Amendment Form available at the following website:

http://www.research.mq.edu.au/current_research_staff/human_research_ethics/managing_approved_research_projects

5.   Please notify the Sub-Committee immediately in the event of any adverse effects on participants or of any unforeseen events that affect the continued ethical acceptability of the project.

6.   At all times you are responsible for the ethical conduct of your research in accordance with the guidelines established by the University. This information is available at the following websites:

http://www.mq.edu.au/policy

http://www.research.mq.edu.au/for/researchers/how_to_obtain_ethics_approval/human_research_ethics/policy

If you will be applying for or have applied for internal or external funding for the above project it is your responsibility to provide the Macquarie University's Research Grants Management Assistant with a copy of this email as soon as possible. Internal and External funding agencies will not be informed that you have approval for your project and funds will not be released until the Research Grants Management Assistant has received a copy of this email.

If you need to provide a hard copy letter of approval to an external organisation as evidence that you have approval, please do not hesitate to contact the Ethics Secretariat at the address below.

Please retain a copy of this email as this is your official notification of ethics approval.

Yours sincerely,

Dr Anthony Miller
Chair
Faculty of Human Sciences
Human Research Ethics Sub-Committee

Faculty of Human Sciences - Ethics
Research Office
C5C-17 Wallys Walk L3
Macquarie University
NSW 2109

Ph: +61 2 9850 4197
Email: fhs.ethics@mq.edu.au
http://www.research.mq.edu.au/

Appendix H

Survey Advertisement

Early Childhood Matters: An exploration of family social media networking experiences

You are invited to participate in a research study exploring parents' experiences of using online social media.

It is hoped that this information can assist early childhood educators develop better relationships when working with families raising children.

Click here to start the survey

By answering all the survey questions, you will go in a draw to win two Gold Class movie tickets to Event Cinemas!

Thank you for forwarding this link to other families you know who are raising children and may also like to participate in this research study.

For more information about the study please contact:
suzana.stipanovic@hdr.mq.edu.au or manjula.waniganayake@mq.edu.au

This study has been approved by the Macquarie University Human Research Ethics Committee (No. 5201600370).
Participate now!
Be in the running for two Gold Class movie tickets!!

Appendix I

Post: daycare

User: RC0117

18/03/2013

hello, my 19 month old daughter is being orientated to a lovely daycare centre, however she screams her head off and gets extremely distressed when i leave her for upto 15 minutes and my nerves feel like they are on fire and i feel like i am about to explode. i usually start crying and have a very strong urge to race back into the room and cuddle my baby and i constantly think that maybe this is wrong despite everyone telling me it is very good for thier socialization...my mother can look after my todler who i still refer to as my bubba as she will always be , when i work but i want a bit of me time, just one morning a week. well as a matter of fact anytime she cries my heart beats fast and i just want to soothe her cuddle her pat her until she calms right down, even sometimes being so soft i let her have a sip of coffee, my car keys .or something i am trying to get off her or persuade her from not doing..i am a first time mum who had very bad poor boundaries from the very beginning feeling my baby and i were one, to the point of finding it hard people i didnt really know or trust hold her..especially if she cried..feeling abit lost, and questioning my mother abilities..even though my husband and mum say i am great, i do question myself and wish maybe i could be a bit firmer and dont want my bubba to be a spoilt child because we are not having anymore due to medical condition...any ideas out there?/ any similar stories about poor boundaries or difficulities starting childcare?/ thankyou

---

RC0092

27/06/2016

May be she needs more time. Let her grow one more year and then think of letting her attend the preschool/daycare.

RC0025

22/06/2016

In my opinion, parents need to take care of their baby for at least 3 years then they could send to daycare. So, I and family used to take care of my baby who is 1.5 years at home only with the use of some child care product that helps us to do other care simultaneously by taking baby care. Like we use travel cot when we plan for any trips. For getting more tips you can visit: http://parentsneed.com/

CPSIA information can be obtained
at www.ICGtesting.com
Printed in the USA
LVHW080550280223
740519LV00015B/267